Community Music in Alberta

Some Good Schoolhouse Stuff!

ROCKY MOUNTAIN FOLK CLUB
Calgary, Alberta

Calgary's Rocky Mountain Folk Club began in 1976 and continues to provide a venue where folk music is performed for a listening yet participating audience. The house band, *Ceard* (pronounced *kay-ard*), opens each Rocky evening (eight to ten Fridays a year) with "Farewell to Nova Scotia" while the audience sings lustily on the chorus. After 45 minutes of songs with the house band, guest musicians take to the stage, and the next two hours are filled with more unique music and fun. The bar opens during intermissions, and the socializing begins. But soon it's back to the performers until the end of the evening when *Ceard* returns to the stage (often assisted by the guests) to lead some unaccompanied traditional songs with everyone on the chorus, finishing off with "Wild Mountain Thyme." Rocky dates and guests are listed in most Calgary entertainment calendars.

Community Music in Alberta has been sponsored by The Rocky Mountain Folk Club.

Community
Music
in Alberta

Some Good Schoolhouse Stuff!

By
George W. Lyon

UC
PRESS

University of Calgary Press
2500 University Drive N.W.
Calgary, Alberta, Canada T2N 1N4

Canadian Cataloguing in Publication Data
Lyon, George W., 1945-
    Community music in Alberta

    Includes bibliographical references and index.
    ISBN 1-895176-83-2

    1. Community music – Alberta – History and criticism. 2. Community music – Alberta
    – Pictorial works I. Title.
ML3563.7.A3L989 1999   780'.97123   C99-910319-9

Front cover photo – PB 769-1, Glenbow Archives.
Inside back cover photo – NA 5265-9, Glenbow Archives (computer alteration by Glenbow).

Book design by Cliff Kadatz.

Printed and bound in Canada by Hignell Book Printing
∞ This book is printed on acid-free paper.

We acknowledge the financial support of the Government of Canada through the Book Publishing Industry Development Program (BPIDP) for our publishing activities.

This is offered to the memory of
Mark B. deLeeuw

—

I don't care what they say;
it was a dumb hobby, kid.

George

Table of Contents

Acknowledgements

began my researches into the cultural history of Alberta in 1985 with the assistance of the Alberta Historical Resources Foundation, who have continued to support my work. My gratitude to Trudy Cowan, Esther Brown, Guan L. Law, and Monika McNabb can never be adequately stated. Important financial support has also come from the Social Sciences and Humanities Research Council of Canada, the Helen Creighton Foundation, and Rāgā Mālā Performing Arts of Canada.

During the decade that has passed, I have had more fascinating and helpful discussions than I can possibly credit here. Let my acknowledgements to Michael Pollock, John Leeder, Esther Brown, Sid Holt, Jennifer Bobrovitch, Jānis Svilpis, Jim Hiscott, Judith Cohen, Donald Deschênes, Laurie Mills, and Edith Fowke demonstrate how widespread and various my cognitive and emotional support has been.

By the same token, I have spoken to too many "informants" (an awkward word for people, some of whom I hope are friends!) to name all of them, much less to acknowledge their contribution to this work. During the summer of 1990, I completed a project entitled Alberta's Musical Elders; during that period I spoke to Joe Mason, Myrtle Holt, Harold Anderson, Jac Friedenberg, Roy and Mildred Logan, and Bud and Charlie Beaton. All of them (and many others) are reflected in these pages; I hope they will be pleased to recognize themselves, even when they are not named. Two summers before that, Tony Neidermayer gave me several precious hours of his life; I hope I have used them well. Martin Rossander, as always, offers me insight, stimulation and fellowship beyond description.

A diligent effort has been made to contact those who created the local histories, whose quotations bring life to this presentation. A few remain elusive; if anyone can direct me to the editors of Cherished Memories, Harvest of Memories, A History of Pioneering in the Pakan District, La Glace Yesterday and Today, Land of the Lakes, Links of Memory, Lone Butte North, Memories of Fairgrove District, Mingling Memories, Olds, Reflections, Ridgewood Community, Trails to the Bow, Wagon Trails Grown Over, or Vermilion Memories, I will be much obliged.

All of the workers, both paid and volunteer, who keep the University of Calgary Press alive during these years of tight money (and, in some circles, tighter hearts) deserve my thanks and yours, as well. We'll hand the roses to Shirley Onn and know that she'll pass them around. As one of the external readers commented, the success of this book will be utterly dependent upon the work of the designer; Cliff Kadatz, take a bow. (By the way—Michael P., thanks again, this time for "Red Wing.")

Richard Johnston and W.A.S. Sarjeant were my reader/editors; they made it a better book.

And without Lois, I don't know how I'd have done it. Sometimes I might not even know why.

Unless otherwise indicated, all place names in this book refer to Alberta locations.

Many of the photographs used for this book come from local histories. These are identified by title in the captions, and bibliographic details for each may be found at the end of the text.

Photographs identified by the letters NA, NB, NC, ND, and PB came from the Glenbow Archives in Calgary. Those prefixed A, B, B1, G, Gs, J, Ks, OB, Os, P, and PA are from the Provincial Archives in Edmonton. Prints of these photos (and thousands of others on hundreds of other subjects) may be purchased from both archives at reasonable prices. These institutions are open to all visitors — they are not forbidding, esoteric sanctums for scholars only. I have always found their staff members to be friendly and helpful; you will, too!

A few photographs came from the artists or subjects themselves, who are identified by name. Any unsigned photos were taken or gathered by the author.

Introduction

Mary Turner came to Spruce View, Alberta, from Texas with her husband William and several other families in 1912.

My husband's three sons were with us, also my son and daughter by a previous marriage. When we were on the road with our wagons nearly two months, we had to set up camp and stay until I gave birth to my baby — a fine big boy. I lay on my carpet in my tent beside a beautiful lake. Not far away was a crowd of people enjoying a grand picnic, and I could hear the fine, sweet music all day and far into the night. **Grub-Axe To Grain.**

When I discovered this passage, early in my study of the local histories of Alberta, I felt that it was among the most moving reminiscences of the experience of listening to music that I'd ever encountered. A decade later, I'm still moved by it, especially when I consider what Ms. Turner heard. The music of that picnic probably began with a brass band, which would have played a variety of marches, hymns, polkas, and popular tunes. In the evening the band may have also played for dancing, but it may have been replaced by a fiddler or two, either unaccompanied or supported by chording on piano, guitar, banjo, or mandolin, or perhaps all of these and more! Her account doesn't say where she had stopped, and the picnickers may or may not have been fellow Texans. They might have been locals; after two months, the emigrants would have been well up the trail, though we don't know whether or not she had crossed the border yet.

Unless her party had camped near a Scandinavian, Dutch, or other European colony, the music Mary Turner enjoyed must have come from the dance repertoire of the British/American fiddle, with some admixture of the popular music of the day. She almost certainly enjoyed "Red Wing" that evening. "Red Wing," a Tin Pan Alley song based upon a central European folk tune, was popular as a singalong number and as accompaniment for the two-step and polka throughout the northern plains; it is cited more often than any other song in the local histories and was popular among homesteading groups. She probably listened to the venerable British reel, "Soldier's Joy," and to its Yankee cousin, "Turkey in the Straw," and possibly to "Sally Goodin" (especially if the picnickers were also from Texas!), to the "Heel and Toe Polka," and to "Put On Your Old Grey Bonnet," written by the ragtime composer Percy Wenrich. Popular religious numbers, which were likely sung while the musicians took breaks, included "Abide With Me," "The Old Rugged Cross," "Nearer, My God, to Thee," and "O God, Our Help in Ages Past." If the community included a resident wag, as most did, he may have attempted to bring the figurative house down with "The Preacher and the Bear" or "The Smoke Went Up the Chimney Just the Same." The picnickers' last dance was almost certainly either "Westphalia Waltz" or, most likely, "Home, Sweet Home," and any upright man would be sure to dance the last waltz with the woman he brought to the dance, be she his wife or a friend.

It might surprise some people that this repertoire would be described as "fine, sweet music." Except for the hymns and possibly the waltzes, our era classifies this music as "good time" stuff: it's fun, noisy, and not to be taken seriously, except when performed with virtuoso technique. But I have long felt that our categories are both too firm and too narrow. If we found some alternatives to gee-hawing and classical snootiness, we might learn to hear this music in the way that Mary Turner heard it.

In some of the social sciences, it is now popular to look closely at "native esthetics": How do the people of a culture react to their own arts? Some groups don't express their esthetic preferences in newspaper reviews or scholarly treatises; this should not be taken as evidence that they lack such preferences or that they cannot give good reasons for those preferences. Anthropologists are interested in native esthetics because they want to understand *other* societies. Mary Turner's brief anecdote might lead us to a better understanding of *our own past* — and consequently of our present.

The passage offers a genuine insight into Mary Turner's world, a world invariably characterized in Alberta by the word "Heritage." "Heritage," like "folklore," is often used to refer to a society that is antique, monolithic, and unchanging. But the music Mary Turner listened to came from a variety of sources and was in the process of change due to immigration and industrialization. In some ways, her world looks remarkably like ours. Are we surprised to find a blended family in her day as in ours? Presumably the interpersonal troubles that we associate with what might be seen as a non-traditional family were also present; our myth of the heritage family may need to be revised.

So may our myth of the hard lives of our provincial ancestors. Surely, travelling while pregnant from Texas to Alberta in a horsedrawn wagon and giving birth in a tent posed difficulties unknown to many of us, even without the stereotypical threats of painted Indians and masked outlaws. But our lives can be difficult, as well, and Ms. Turner hardly seems to plead for sympathy. Difficulties are the human lot and only become traumatic when our society fails to support us. The "fine, sweet music" that cheered Ms. Turner in her evening of productive pain was one aspect of a functioning social network. To speak of early Albertans as "pioneers" who "had little time for culture," a conclusion commonly drawn, is to apply an outdated definition of culture and to patronize Mary Turner and her contemporaries.

Obviously these pages can contain no music, though to those of us who've listened widely to the still living traditions which the photographs document (some of them portray musicians you may still hear in western Canada), there are vibrant, if faint, echoes that emerge from the halftone dots. But though the photos cannot give us the sound of the music, they show us, over and over again, how important music has been in the social and private lives of Albertans, how important culture has always been in the province.

The cultural history of Alberta is considerably more varied than is often credited. Neither the past nor the future is served by excessive stereotyping of the province's antique culture. Mary Turner's memoir reminds us that our understanding of the variety of the province's musical past must begin with a recognition that the musical experience is always tied to the social, economic, political, and personal dimensions of life, as it alerts us that we might learn to listen to music in new ways. The photographs presented here reveal that there has always been an abundance of musical styles, genres, and situations in Alberta.

This is not a history of music in the province. No one I'm aware of is in a position to write such a book, which would have to be very long and complicated because the interactions among the genres and idioms of music in this province's century have been quite complex. These different musics have sometimes outshouted each other and sometimes gone their independent ways, but rarely have they ignored each other. It is not coincidental, for example, that both country music (including the cowboy poetry movement) and the Pow Wow circuit have undergone noticeable revival of older styles of dress and music during the last decade or so. Nor should we be surprised that the rhythm section of polka, country, and rock bands are identical and that the techniques used to play some of these instruments may not vary substantially. This does not mean that these are not independent genres — just ask most of the fans of each! — but it does demonstrate that distinct cultures share a common world.

The photos in this album portray both continuity and change. Fiddling, for example, was perhaps the oldest European musical tradition to be established in western Canada, but fiddle *contests* are relatively new. The **Calgary Herald** and the Stampede sponsored successful contests in the twenties, which attracted overflow crowds to the Grand Theatre, but the institution did not become widespread until the 1980s. Why? Perhaps fiddle contests have grown as the fiddle became less important in dance music. Most of the old time tunes that are featured in contests — jigs and reels in particular, but also waltzes and other genres — were once important accompaniments to dances which are no longer widely popular.

In some cases, young men who'd gotten involved in careers on the farm or elsewhere put aside the instrument with maturity, as one puts aside many of the pleasures of youth. While they were away from music, the fiddle became less essential at dances, which came to require the trumpet, the saxophone, and, with the advent of amplification, the guitar.

Entering the retirement culture that came into existence after World War II, many of these people found themselves with free time. Not all of them were able to return to the dance floor, but some rediscovered the delight they had taken in music as youngsters.

For instance, Elmer Bolinger, of Gleichen, had taken lessons on the violin in Calgary as a high school student (indeed, he studied under Mary Shortt, who was the first teacher of many *classical* violinists, some of whom went on to professional careers). During these years he played for dance bands in town and country. After his life as a farmer, when the violin sat in its case in a closet while the harvests, holdings, and house grew larger, he wandered into a fiddle contest with his wife Ralphene, to whom he commented on his way out, "You know, that looks like fun. I believe I'll give it a try." With Ralphene accompanying him on piano, he became a frequent winner in the Senior category. Like quite a few of their generation and younger folks, as well, they took fiddling vacations, entering contests as far south as Yuma, Arizona.

The interaction between continuity and change involves the First Nations of Alberta, as well as immigrants. I have put the Native people at the end of this book, in order to emphasize their dynamic role in this process. The music of Alberta doesn't merely *begin* with the Native people, it *continues* with them. During earlier incarnations (as illustration to a magazine article and as a travelling exhibit), this presentation repeated the standard procedure by beginning the account with Natives, since, after all, they *were* here first, but after these perfunctory nods, leaving them behind, stuck in ancient history as the Vanishing Redman.

However, after living with this material for many years, I've come to find this approach less satisfying. Native people are not vanishing; quite the opposite! Neither is their culture a thing of the past, unrelated to the rest of the world. True, there are portions of it which they carefully preserve for their own uses; all cultures have areas where they attempt to minimize change, especially when it comes to religious ritual. But the very existence of the Pow Wow circuit is testimony to cultural change; Pow Wow is often spoken of as a "Pan-Indian" cultural institution, a creator of unity. Where once Native people conceived of themselves as Siksika, Cree, Tsuu T'ina, or other nationalities, the arrival of Europeans taught them to understand themselves as "Indians." As the social and economic circumstances threatened (or at least altered) certain cultural situations, the Pow Wow made it possible to reconceive many of these events as social occasions. As with fiddling, the contest situation provided a new context for old customs, which invariably change with the context. Contest fiddling and chicken dancing have become complex displays of virtuoso competence which might have been inappropriate in older worlds.

The arrival of the Europeans brought new materials, sometimes new instruments, and probably new esthetic visions to the Native people. The jingle dress, for example, is a modern development from older garments decorated with animal teeth and other natural objects which would make a pleasant sound when the wearer moved. But now the jingling cone is bent from metal, often from something originally as inelegant as a snuff tin, and its tinkle differs from the organic rustle of elk teeth or deer dew claws. Indeed, this "light metal" sound suits well the shiny, sparkly space age fabric that jingle-dress dancers sometimes favor. Perhaps in reaction to this almost futuristic "Fancy Dance" outfit (there are male Fancy Dancers, as well as female), many Natives have moved back to "Traditional Dance" outfits, which, despite their name, are *not* simply clones of the styles of pre-contact Native cultures. These, too, show *development* of older designs, often demonstrating a complexity that makes the most baroque designs of the fifties pale in comparison.

It cannot be an accident that something similar is occurring in country music; one can hear, for example, considerable influence from such earlier singers as Lefty Frizzell and Loretta Lynn in the styles of such "new traditionalists" as George Fox and Cindy Church, but the melisma those earlier singers brought to country music has been exaggerated among many of the new singers to the point that one is often tempted to use the term "arabesque" to describe it. It seems that we live in an era when many cultures reward the ability to produce complex demonstrations of carefully practiced skills.

But we should not forget that it can take as much skill to produce a graceful, simple melody or dance as it does to produce a complicated one. Nor should we assume that older generations of Albertans lacked the skills or training to produce artistic complexity. True, professionalism brings with it a degree of skill development that isn't possible on a part time basis, but we would be foolish indeed to think that our music is "better" or "more complex" than that of older eras. The photographs in this collection demonstrate that the musical history of Alberta was varied; it is unfortunate that so little of it was recorded, for actually to hear the music would allow us to say more about its complexity in earlier years.

What the many diverse musical styles portrayed in these pages have in common is that all of them have been *performed* in Alberta by Albertans. My selection has favored the nonprofessional performances of local musicians, but I have not ignored professional performers who have toured the province, the region, and beyond. Some non-Albertans also appear in these pages because this provincial culture has always grown in the context of a larger world. This explains the "Alberta" of my title. Although I'm not pretending to offer a *history*, this survey is "historic" in its focus. Generally, my survey ends with the sixties; I do not look for new trends after that period, except for the fiddle contest circuit and a few aspects of music among Native Albertans.

I call all of this "community music," in part to avoid the terms "folk," "popular," and "classical" because in this case I am more interested in what the musics made by Albertans have in common than in categorizing them. We find instances of all of these cultural modes here. As I use the terms, "folk" music refers to noncommercial music performed by and for members of a small group. This definition excludes such Albertans as James Keelaghan and Jann Arden, who are often called "folksingers," because these performers are attempting to earn their living through their music and therefore go beyond their own friends and neighbors for their audiences. "Popular" music, which includes those performers as well as many night club entertainers, rock bands, and so on, refers, then, to music made, generally, by professionals. "Classical" music is also often made by professionals, but these professionals restrict themselves to the repertoire and techniques of musically literate, usually very profound, composers, most of whom are European.

This is a thumbnail distinction among these musical modes. We needn't bother with more precision here, simply because our story is about how they have worked together, not about the tensions between them. It might surprise some readers that "classical" music has a long and significant history in Alberta; I've capitalized upon that surprise by considering that mode early in our survey, rather than beginning with Native culture or with folk music, as is commonly done. Whether the first music performed in Alberta by European Canadians was folk, popular, or classical really matters very little; the difference was a matter of months. Among the earliest settlers were people with a love for, and training in, the classical music of Europe, fiddlers who knew scores of reels and jigs (or workingmen with risqué ballads), and pianists who brought the sheet music to the latest Tin Pan Alley hits.

The subtitle of this work comes from an exclamation made by Martin Rossander, who has written several essays on the music he remembers from Alberta in the thirties and whose picture from those days appears on page 111 (Figure 236). Once, while visiting at my house, he wandered into the living room as I played a record by the Saskatchewan group, Grand Coulee Old Tyme Jug Band. He listened intently for a moment and then smiled, "That's some good school-house stuff!"

Much of this schoolhouse stuff is often called "old time music," but that term also means different things depending upon locale and era. From the peoples of Britain came the sources of many Canadian old time musics: the fiddle and bagpipe music and ballads from ancient days. In the southern mountains of the U.S., this music resurfaced in the fiddle and banjo, in the styles from which bluegrass was created. Mention of the banjo (now an instrument commonly found in Alberta, as throughout the world), reminds us of another great source for old time music, Africa. Though it has by mistake been called an "original" American instrument, the banjo came to this continent from Africa, a continent which has had a significant cultural impact upon the Americas. If you go to the predominantly African American areas along the Mississippi River, old time music is the bottleneck guitar blues of the jook joints and barrelhouses, but musical ideas and attitudes from African America have reached nearly every corner of the continent. British and African music, influenced by various other cultures combined to form the great North American musical traditions which have swept the world during this century: jazz, country and western, and rock and roll. Today, these genres dominate the musical horizon in Alberta as elsewhere.

Canadian folk music is often identified with the old time musics of Quebec, Ontario, and the Maritimes, each of which has its own flavor. The music of the prairies has been a well kept secret; indeed, many folklorists have doubted the existence of any indigenous folk culture on the prairies. Western Canada is a large region, and it was populated by many groups, each of whom brought their own ingredients. To the British root stock was grafted the Norwegian *hoppwaltz*, the Ukrainian *kolomayka*, and the *polkas* of many nations. Since much of the settlement of the prairies occurred during the twentieth century, modern communications have brought in such influences as Edith Piaf's Parisian torch songs, the jazz of New York and Chicago, and the rock of Memphis. And there has always been classical music on the prairies.

A few examples of Alberta old time music from my own experience:

a Blackfoot fiddler exploring two phrases of "When My Blue Moon Turns To Gold Again" in an unusual time signature,

the saxes and piano at the Wednesday afternoon dance at the Kerby Senior Centre in Calgary ripping into the old Everly Brothers hit, "Bye Bye Love,"

a recording of Franz Liszt's "Liebestraum" played by tenor-banjoist Ray Little, accompanied by his country and western band,

and a cut-up named Barney (I wish I had gotten his last name!) winding out a lonesome rendition of "Lili Marlene" on piano accordion at a seniors' Halloween party in a city community centre.

There are many figures who could qualify as stars of Alberta community music; I wish I could portray them all, but there isn't space even to name them. Roy Logan and his Orchestra will have to stand for so many others. This ensemble played for dances at the Fifty And Over Club in Calgary for nearly forty years, every Monday night, except for summer and holidays. That's a pretty heroic engagement. Their music was vigorous, elegant, and humorous, and it emerged from the schoolhouses of Alberta. It was an Alberta music; you'll never hear anything like it in Quebec or Newfoundland, or in Nashville, either. To play for dancers, you've got to have your act together. Of course, your time's got to be accurate, so people don't get their feet tripped up, but if your dancers are really going to enjoy themselves, you've also got to be able to give it some swing, some personality.

Logan, the first child born at the new hospital in Bassano in 1916, lived in several different regions of Alberta; he began playing for dances when he was twelve years old. His father, who wasn't a musician himself, recognized the value of music and so brought home some instruments for the children and unknowingly set the course of Logan's life. "Thank goodness my father got those instruments!" This regard for music was maintained in the Logan family: in order to purchase a piano for their own children, Roy's wife Mildred knit socks, which Roy sold around Calgary. As the children began to play the instrument, Mildred, herself a pianist, shifted to the drums, so that she could play along.

Roy met Hugh Carlson, a fiddler/pianist from Delburne, at a jam session in the English town of Digby, Lincolnshire, during World War Two. When the men returned to Calgary after the war, they looked each other up. Carlson had come from a musical family; his parents (father a fiddler, mother a pianist) were constantly in demand for dances. Hugh had begun to learn to fiddle by his sixth year. Frustrated by the large size of his father's instrument, he was surprised one Christmas with a smaller instrument that he could handle. From his father, he learned some of the old time repertoire, items like "Buffalo Gals" and, of course, "Red Wing." Naturally, as a young man in this century, his heart was taken by popular dance music, tunes like "Five Foot Two" and "Little White Lies."

In Calgary after the war, Carlson played some dances with the legendary Ma Trainor, and he and Logan worked in a group called The Gay Fifties, which played for a seniors' club. Despite the title, and despite the club rule that to attend a dance you had to be over fifty years of age, neither Carlson nor Logan had reached their fiftieth birthdays yet!

The Fifty and Over Club, for which the Logan Orchestra was the house band, was founded in 1957. When Carlson got a day job with a shift that prevented him from making the gig, John and Myrtle Holt joined the group. John, a professor of civil engineering by trade, was a multi-instrumentalist; Myrtle played keyboards. When John died in the 1980s, Carlson returned to the Orchestra.

Myrtle Holt also came from a musical family and has performed all of her life. She studied a variety of instruments as a child, both formally and informally, including several years as a music student at Mount Royal College. She has taught guitar, organ, piano, banjo, and accordion, and has played in western, Scottish, Swedish, and Norwegian ensembles, as well as in popular and old time dance orchestras.

Myrtle is the only member of the Orchestra who had much formal training. Hugh taught himself saxophone during the fifties, with the help of a few lessons, "... the only lessons I ever took in my life." Nevertheless, when Roy took his children and grandchildren to their music lessons, he paid close attention to the instruction they received and believed that his own musicianship benefitted from this secondhand instruction.

Members of the Logan Orchestra performed singly and in other combinations. Roy was extremely active on the fiddle contest scene; when I last spoke to him, he had over ninety trophies — by his death in 1998, it was over a hundred! Myrtle and Hugh have also fronted their own groups; Myrtle's is the Versatiles and Hugh's was the Carlson Orchestra. (Hugh also died in 1998.) "Sometimes it's kind of hectic," Myrtle acknowledges. So much for the idea that old time music doesn't thrive in contemporary Calgary.

The Logan Orchestra repertoire ranged from such old time staples as "The Spanish Waltz" and "Red River Valley" through Swing Era favorites like "Somebody Stole My Gal" and "Just Because" to country and western hits, "Okie From Muskogee" and "Faded Love." Their musical personality was enhanced by the versatility of the group's members. Mildred Logan maintained the rhythm, and Hugh Carlson and Roy doubled on fiddle and piano, while Myrtle Holt switched between accordion and piano. The band's front, then, might have been two fiddles and piano or accordion or fiddle, piano, and accordion. These changes were often the occasion for the banter that characterized the group's performances. Once, as Logan moved over to the piano, he turned to someone near the stage and said, "I'm not really very good, but don't tell everyone." Carlson, delighted with the opening his friend had provided, added, "They'll hear it themselves!"

The Logan Orchestra drew crowds to the West Mount Pleasant Community Hall for four decades with their combination of humor, elegance, and rhythm. Their repertoire and personality demonstrated how community music survived and flourished by choosing carefully from the palette of musical possibilities from the past and the present.

Some very good schoolhouse stuff, even in the nineties!

One of the first orders of the day...

One of the first orders of the day for settlers on the prairies was the creation of the school district. There was a board to be elected, land to be set aside, taxes to allocate, a schoolhouse to be constructed, and a teacher to be hired. The schoolhouse became the location for a variety of essential social, cultural, and spiritual activities.

Our schoolhouse was certainly the centre of community life for many years. I remember with what special excitement the older pupils would say on a Friday afternoon, 'There is going to be a dance here tonight!' Teacher would tell us to take our books and pencils out of our desks and put them in one special corner with the teacher's desk. Then if I was lucky enough to come to the dance, what a thrill to walk in and see an unfamiliar room, all empty of furniture, the desks piled row on row against the window side of the school and crude benches along the other walls....

The dances were so different from what they are today. Which of our children have seen the grace and beauty of a roomful of couples, all in regular line, dancing the beautiful four-step? What of the dainty French Minuet, the militarily precise three-step, and the joyous and bouncy Cabbage-dance direct from the Ukraine?

... By the time I had grown to the age of having boyfriends, there were community halls where the newer dances were held. Somehow the grace of those earlier days was lost and with the old faces leaving, and the old dances too, much of the enjoyment was lost to me, and I turned to other things. Caroline Relf, **Building and Working Together.**

And the parties and dances. How did so many get into such a small room? Desks piled against walls where we kids sat watching the adults doing the Lancers and 'Gents bow low' and catching exciting glimpses of the teacher's petticoats as the men swung the girls off their feet. Cy Arkinstall, I think it was, played the fiddle. The two Arkinstall girls, fine Scots dancers, doing the Schottische. The men getting warmer and warmer — going outside to smoke between dances and putting the cigarette behind their ears when the dance resumed. Since the cigarette often got sweat soaked and non-smokeable until dried, it often

Figure 1 – Dundee School, 1930s.

NA 5597-23

finished on the window ledge where we kids rescued it and learnt the taste of cigarettes next school day.

Then the concerts. Dr. Wickers singing 'Angus MacDonald Come Home From The Wars'; Mrs. A.D. Carmichael, 'My Ain Folk' and 'There's a Wee Hoose 'Mang the Heather'; my mother singing 'Fiddle and I'; Annie Carmichael, 'Comin' Through the Rye'; Mrs. Moody Wilson with her tremendous accompaniments. Then there were recitations and monologues — but the music has remained with me best." **Memories of Fairgrove District.**

The schoolhouse sometimes resembled a church, (Fig. 2), and this pleasant coincidence should remind us that the schoolhouse often served as a church until one was built or until a new denomination developed a large enough congregation to afford its own meeting house. (Fig. 3).

In those days there was one minister to serve several districts, and until I went away to high school, I used to go with him on Sundays to play the piano. Fortunately, most country schools had either an organ or piano. Edna (McFadden) Dick, **Wheat Country.**

I remember Mr. Wilkinson, the Anglican minister, being at a Patriotic Society concert at a nearby country school. After the concert and lunch were over, the younger people quite naturally wanted to dance away what remained of the night. One older woman among those present objected very strongly to this because, she said, it would be disrespectful to the 'cloth.' Mr. Wilkinson noted the disturbance at the dishwashing area, where this one lady upheld her objections to the dance, and asked a schoolboy what was upsetting the ladies. 'The old one,' answered the boy, 'says it ain't proper to dance where there's a preacher.' Mr. Wilkinson moved to the piano, sat down on the stool, called out loudly, 'Everybody waltz!' and began to play. Mrs. Robert Mailer, **Shortgrass Country.**

Of course, churches eventually built annexes to provide sites for dances and other cultural activities, as well. We should also remember that singing during the church service provided many Albertans with a significant cultural experience, especially those who felt that their singing voices were not good enough to exhibit on any other occasion.

Another location for music, then as now, was the hotel's tavern and ballroom, if there was one (Fig. 4).

Once the King George Hotel was built, many stayed there overnight to attend the big dances which followed the all day baseball tournaments. Before that people danced until dawn to avoid going home in the dark ... and before that gatherings were limited to homefolds and neighbors. **Fencelines and Furrows.**

Figure 2 – Public school, Leduc (1906).

Figure 3 – Leduc (1906).

Figure 4 – 1912.

Figure 5

NA 5125-1

Figure 6 – Christmas night dance at Robinson's Hall, Calgary, 1913.
Robinson's Hall later became Penley's Academy, a major dance studio and ballroom in Calgary.

As Albertans prospered, they built community halls, both publicly owned...(Fig. 5).

Having paid the pipers, some community members felt entitled to call the tune. Excerpts from a Clyde Community Hall meeting on August 29, 1939:
Recommendations to the orchestra — that the orchestra at present is not very well balanced — the banjo drowning out the guitar, and the saxophone player drowning out the other instruments. We suggest the saxophone player should tone down; another violin player would be more effective than guitar. **80 Years of Progress.**

...and privately (Fig. 6).

So the story of Alberta's music during its first century properly begins in the schoolhouse, where Albertans came to dance and pray on the weekends. During the week, of course, young Albertans occupied the building and often learned music there.

Through school instruction, school concerts, and the often school-related music festivals, Albertans learned techniques, repertoire, and attitudes towards music. It may be that some music education tended to work against local traditions, causing Albertans to value practices and skills from elsewhere more than those of local musicians, but the skills and experiences many gained at school were invaluable.

*In the winter time there was hardly a noon hour would go by that we didn't push the desks back and crank up the record player, and teachers and students both would square dance the noon hour away. I don't think there was a kid from grade one up that didn't know how to dance. Linda Rollins, **Wagon Trails Grown Over.***

In 1914, the Paramount School opened; Miss Mable Eng, who was 18 years old at the time, was the first teacher. "Miss Eng had a hard time controlling us, being not much older than many of the students. The Jepson boys' father, Marinius, was on the school board and decided to pay a surprise visit to us one afternoon about two o'clock. When he arrived,

Land of Red and White

Figure 7 – Frog Lake School Orchestra 1937. Did the teacher at the Frog Lake School in 1937 teach all of these instruments? Perhaps, but perhaps the students got some pointers at home, too.

G1448

Figure 8 – H.A. Kostash School band, Smoky Lake, May 12, 1950. (The extensive photographic record of the Smoky Lake area created by Nicholas Gavinchuk provides a northern counterpart to the legacy of Thomas Gushul from the Crowsnest Pass. Alberta has been blessed with a number of fine photographers, professional and private, during its short history.)

PA 1309/2

Figure 9 – School orchestra in Edmonton, January 1960.

NA 4093-41

Figure 10 – Nordegg, ca. 1913.

A7100

Figure 11 – Rhythm band in a one-room schoolhouse, Wheatland, late forties.

a dance was in full progress. I was playing the mouth organ, and the other students were singing along as they danced, and right in the centre of it all was Miss Eng dancing up a storm with one of the older boys. Mr. Jepson was very angry and finished off the blast that followed with 'I knew my boys didn't know anything, but now I have a good idea why.' Miss Eng was replaced the next year by Bill Hustler who taught for the next two terms, 1915 and 1916. He was an excellent teacher and certainly had his work cut out for him trying to smarten us all up. A.J. Bartling, **Reflections**.

The basic rhythm band, cheaply supplied, was a schoolhouse staple, which often led to more elaborate musical studies. (Fig. 11)

Figure 12 – Smoky Lake School, December 21, 1951.

Figure 13 – Christmas wasn't the only occasion for such glamorous gatherings; Halloween Party, Smoky Lake School, October 31, 1951.

Figure 14 – Halloween Party, Smoky Lake School, October 31, 1951.

Figure 15 – Smoky Lake, 1950.

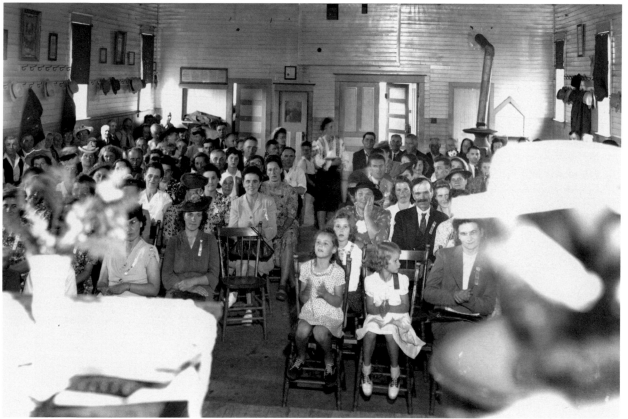

Figure 16 – Smoky Lake, 1946.

Figure 17 – Nick Myshok performs at his high school graduation
in Mundare, probably during the forties.

*During the late thirties, Baker School had a
musical group which played on tin whistles
and percussion instruments made from such
homely objects as jam lids, &c. "Why, we
almost won first prize at a festival, but were
narrowly defeated by a mandolin orchestra
playing expensive 'store-bought' instruments.
We might have won that, if the sharp-eyed
adjudicator hadn't spotted one little girl with
absolutely no sense of rhythm who was supposed to be in the back row, but had somehow
got squeezed to the front." David J. Wright.*
Cherished Memories*.*

Particularly talented students are singled out and
given the chance to display their achievement. For
many Albertans the experience of performance
begins and ends (alas!) at school (Fig. 17).

The Christmas concert was perhaps the most
celebrated of community entertainments. While
customs and attitudes varied from district to district,
the concert was frequently considered an integral part
of the curriculum, and teachers might be evaluated
largely on the basis of their concerts. These events
were eagerly awaited throughout the year. Andy
Russell writes that, as a young cowboy, he rode with
his chums around windswept south during December,
attending a different concert each night.

The stagecraft for schoolhouse performances
might have been basic, but even then, the concerts
were carefully rehearsed (Fig. 10). More often, the
big night featured decorated schools and auditori-
ums, beautifully dressed, anxious children, and
eager audiences (Fig. 11-15).

The range of elaboration in these productions
can be seen in the costumes for two versions of the
venerable Robin Hood theme (Fig. 18-19).

Figure 18 – Lead roles in an elaborate Robin Hood play at Wainwright, 1915.

Figure 19 – Younger students, simpler costumes, but there's no less enthusiasm
in this Robin Hood performance at Drumheller, 1925.

The Pekisko Kids

When Doug Stevenson sang "Leave Those Dishes in the Sink, Maw" or "Pass the Biscuits, Mirandy," Babe Hallett leaned even further backward and pulled his accordion even wider, and then when Ab Arnold's smile grew more relaxed, then the Pekisko Kids were really swinging – and so were the dancers!

They started playing first in one another's homes just for the fun of it, and in the fall of 1946 began playing together. Their first engagement was at Pekisko Hall (Fosk-Springdale), so they decided to call themselves The Pekisko Kids. The six original players were Doug Stevenson, Shorty Hanson, Ab and Gordon Arnold, Babe Hallett and Verne Shantz. Morley Scobie and Dick Dayment joined six months later. [Others who have played with the Pekisko Kids are Joan Fox and Dan Dale.] When Doug moved away Ben Buchard and Fred Norton came in.

The boys cut a wide swath over the years playing for more than 400 dances over a twenty year period. Often they played for as many as three dances a week, and the territory they covered was terrific. They played at Calgary, and north of Calgary, south to Lethbridge, east to Reid Hill and Queenstown, and west to Radium Hot Springs – and dozens of places in between. They weren't mercenary. If a dance was of a benefit nature – or the wedding or anniversary of someone they knew – or some special event in their own community – the boys supplied music for free. As Babe said, "Money made little difference to us. We loved to make music and be one of the party."

As well as at Pekisko Hall, they played at Cayley, High River, Nanton, Meadowbank, East Longview, Longview, Black Diamond, Royalties, Parkland, Stavely, Brant, Blackie, Willow Creek, Gladys Ridge, the Stampeder Hotel in Calgary, and at other centres as well. Rodeo dances were a specialty, and so were barn dances, which included the A7 Ranche, the OH, Buster Monkman's, Kentucky, Stampede and dePaoli Ranches.

Ab, Dick and Ben kept the jewellers in High River in business supplying them with picks for their instruments, and Babe went through three accordions – one being pulled apart at one of the early dances at Pekisko.

The band members wore western suits and cowboy hats, but no sequins or splash of any kind, for they were never show-offs. There was nothing artificial about them – they were genuine.

The Pekisko Kids are unique in more ways than one – but one stands out especially. They are probably the only semi-professional dance band who play only by ear. They never used or needed a sheet of music and couldn't have read it if they'd had it. The Little Brown Jug in the corner was the only music they needed. At first they had a problem keeping up with the latest western and dance tunes, but they solved it by gathering in the St. George Coffee Shop in High River with enough nickels to play the latest tune over and over on the Wurlitzer until they had it – note, word and beat. When times became a little more prosperous, they bought a portable record player which enabled them to learn and practise the new tunes in their homes. Frequently someone would request a new number at a dance. If Ab could whistle it a bit, he'd say "Yeh – I know the one you mean – We'll fool around with it and maybe we'll be able to play it yet tonight". And sure enough they would. Everyone whoever danced to the Pekisko Kids remembers how the music would stop and Ab would say "That was purty good. We'll have another spasm," and away they'd go again.

Doug Stevenson was the first leader. He was a lanky young fellow from Saskatchewan with a friendly grin and a drawl that reminded one of the mountains of Tennessee. When Doug left, Ab became the leader.

In all the years of playing it would be hard to pick one night that was a greater triumph than the rest – unless perhaps it was the time that someone tried to add injury to insult by nabbing the Pekisko's own public

address system and placing it at the disposal of an imported band at a High River carnival – and at the same time banishing the Kids to the old Town Hall to make music for any overflow crowd while the imports played for the main carnival. The way it turned out the whole crowd overflowed to the Town Hall and the imported musicians played to a handful of dancers.

The only humiliating experience they ever had was in the 1950's when they were invited to play for a teen-dance at Western Canada High School in Calgary and were to alternate numbers with a Calgary dance band. When the Calgary musicians swung into their groovy rhythms the floor was crowded with jiving teenagers. But when the Pekisko Kids came on with their western brand of music, those dumb city kids just stood and looked. Not one couple ventured on the floor. The boys felt it a crushing snub, but enthusiastic country crowds soon restored their morale.

Often they talked of packing it up, for those late nights were hard to take when they had to work the next day – but someone or something always persuaded them to keep going.

When rodeo and stampede time rolls around each summer, the Pekisko Kids prepare a comic western float for the parade circuit. They have a big collection of ribbons, prizes and trophies as evidence of their success in this line of endeavor. Some of the ideas which they have worked into prize-winning floats are "Saturday Night at Guy Weadick's," "The Lost Lemon Mine," "Medicine Tree and Medicine Wagon," "The Little Red School House and the Still on the Hill," "The Cartwrights of the Ponderosa," "The Buffalo Jump," and "Dingman No.1 Oil Rig." Chris Jensen and his four big greys have an annual contract to pull the Pekisko Kids float. As soon as one stampede is over, Ab starts dreaming up ideas for next year's float.

Babe Hallett moved from Cayley in 1966, making a satisfactory band difficult to get together, but all the old originals, including Doug who came from the northern part of the province, and Dick who came from Salt Springs Island, B.C., assembled again to play for Ab's daughter's wedding dance. None of the old touch was lost – in fact their music was just as good to dance to, and even better for listening, than it had been twenty years before!

Under the Chinook Arch.
Cayley Women's Institute, 1967.

Under the Chinook Arch

Figure 20

Tempting as it may be to assume...

Tempting as it may be to assume that Albertans of earlier years were starved for entertainment, this isn't true. Obviously, they did not have television or movie theatres in every town, but they were visited by various sorts of touring companies, most notably the Chautauqua, which brought them entertainment that was uplifting and enjoyable (Fig. 21)...

...sometimes exotic (Figs. 22, 23)...

...frequently elegant (Figs. 24, 25)...

...and usually capable of teasing the locals with an impression of a glamorous world of sophisticated and cultured people, existing somewhere outside of Alberta (Fig. 26).

But Albertans did not simply rely upon the appearance of travelling professionals. They also mounted their own productions, not only in large centres like Calgary and Edmonton.

Not surprisingly, homegrown entertainments often interpreted themes near to hand: rural life (especially the glamorous cowboy motif) (Fig. 28) or the European heritages of settlers. (Fig. 29)

NA 1900-14

Figure 21 – Chautauqua tent, 1920s.

NA 1900-30

Figure 22 – Albert Vierra's Hawaiian Co., touring western Canada with Chautauqua, 1920s. The strange guitar, second from left, has a number of added bass strings; it's not a common instrument in Hawaiian (or any other) music. The small guitars, known as *ukuleles*, and the slide-fretted lap guitar (at centre) are essential to the Hawaiian sound, a genre that remains influential in many North American folk and popular musics. We'll encounter both lap ("Hawaiian") guitar and ukulele again in our survey.

THE CHAUTAUQUA ORCHESTRA

As a musical program feature of Chautauqua, nothing could be more designed to create the most roseate anticipation than the coming of The Chautauqua Orchestra. To hear these superb musicians is not only to experience the utmost possibilities of a symphonic ensemble, but magnifies one's appreciation of the very best that music affords. These musicians are favorites of many years standing, having played repeatedly before enraptured throngs at the largest Chautauqua assemblies in America. The Chautauqua Orchestra appears in joint concert with Miss Olive McCormick, prima donna soprano, formerly soloist with the Pittsburg Symphony Orchestra.

Olive McCormick

Miss Olive McCormick, coloratura soprano, formerly soloist with the Pittsburg Symphony Orchestra, has been secured for Chautauqua in joint concert with The Chautauqua Orchestra. It is a rare thing to hear a singer so musically satisfying in all registers. Whether a selection is a Tetrazzini operatic favorite, or a tender lullaby, she sings it with exquisite grace, simplicity, and artistic sentiment.

Dr. A. D. Carpenter

The late astronomer, Percival Lowell, founder of the great Lowell Observatory, said: "Dr. Arthur D. Carpenter, the eminent scientist, has performed an invaluable public service in his lectures on astronomy."

In language as thoroughly understandable to children as to adults, Dr. Carpenter illustrates celestial mechanics on his famous Matlick Tellurian machine, a revolving miniature of the universe.

NA 3762-5

Figure 23 – Advertisement for a Chautauqua troupe that performed in Cayley in 1917.

Figure 24 – A Filipino string quartet which also toured the Chautauqua circuit during the 1930s. Filipino string band music, highly influenced by Spanish music, has never been as widely known outside its homeground as are the guitars of Hawaii.

Figure 26 –A Chautauqua troupe preparing to leave Fairview, 1930.

Figure 25 – The Petrie Quartet, Chataugua performances, 1930.

NA 4447-3

Figure 27 – The Pincher Creek Opera Society going on the road in 1911. They were headed for Fort Macleod, where they put on *The Belle of Barnstapoole*.

NA 1869-9

Figure 28 – Cast of **The Highwood Trail** at the Grand Theatre, Calgary, 1923. The play was written by Stampede impresario Guy Weadick, with music by Jack Bullough.

B7235

Figure 29 – Cast of a Ukrainian performance in north/central Alberta from 1918.

NA 3018-68

Figure 30 – Variety Concert in Trochu, 1950.

G1658

Figure 31 – Christmas Concert, Smoky Lake School, December 21, 1951.

A less tasteful entertainment, though it was considered harmless in its day, was the blackface minstrel show. The genre was extremely popular for over a century, throughout this continent and abroad, and did produce some exquisite music, including the songs of Stephen C. Foster. Minstrelsy was an early stage in the interaction of African and European culture on this continent, an interaction that has continued through the Jazz Age into contemporary Country and Rock musics. Although the burnt-cork-and-ham-grease masks have been left behind, it's not certain that more recent performers always escape stereotype — consider, for example, suburban white versions of rap hits.

Asian Albertans have maintained and developed their cultures on this continent. European Albertans, if they have heard music of Asians and Asian Canadians at all, have only heard the processional

NA 1497-9

Figure 32 — Parade in Calgary, 1905.

Na 2622-31

Figure 33 — Parades in Calgary, early 1900s.

NA 3-734

Figure 34 – Cast of The Geisha Girl, probably in Edmonton, 1920.

music of the Chinese New Year or other occasional celebrations (Fig. 32, 33).

But this hasn't prevented them from imagining what this music might sound like — sometimes with peculiar results (Fig. 34).

Of course, not all provincial music theatre has been restricted to such themes. Indeed, the variety of performances throughout Alberta history has been as astonishing as the care and expense that has often gone into the staging of opera, operetta, and musical theatre, even in some rural districts.

NA 3430-15

Figure 35 — Walter Gooder in his dashing costume for the Olds production of H.M.S. Pinafore.

NA 1815-1

Figure 36 — The occasion of this performance is long lost (the photograph is from Calgary, 1899), but the mood of dressup and elegance would appeal to young girls, even a century later.

NA 3430-14

Figure 37 — A performance of **H.M.S. Pinafore** at the town of Olds, ca. 1916.

NA 1852-1

Figure 38 — Women members of the Calgary Light Opera Company, in costume for **H.M.S. Pinafore**, 1897.

Figure 39 – Cast of Hulda of Holland, a production of the Hillspring Opera Company in 1929. At about the same time as their staging of Hulda of Holland, the group also mounted The Outlaw, which they advertised as "Ye Olde English Version...THREE ACT DRAMA...Fast Moving Comedy of Robin Hood and his Merry Men"; the Robin Hood motif was apparently rather popular here in those days.

Such ambitious and sophisticated stagecraft belies the stereotype of the historical rural Albertan as rough and uninterested in sophisticated culture. This is an image the province can outgrow (Fig. 40).

Figure 40 – Petroleum Workers, Turner Valley, 1936.

21

The following two images I've often used to dispel the image of nineteenth-century Albertans as rude pioneers. Both come from the local history, **Donalda's Roots and Branches**. Figure 42 shows a Norwegian family, the Stanviks, at their European home, just prior to emigration in 1891. Figure 41 shows the interior of an Albertan home at roughly the same time. What does the term "frontier" imply? Log Cabins? If so, it appears that the frontier was in Europe! Of course, not all homes in the province were — or are — so elegant as this. The point remains: settlers came to Alberta because they supposed it a place where they might improve their lot, not to live in log cabins.

Figure 41 – Mina Duklet, 1910. Ms. Duklet paid for the organ by doing housework.

Donalda's Roots and Branches

Figure 42 – Notice the zither held by the man at the left.
One supposes this instrument came to Alberta with the family.

Donalda's Roots and Branches

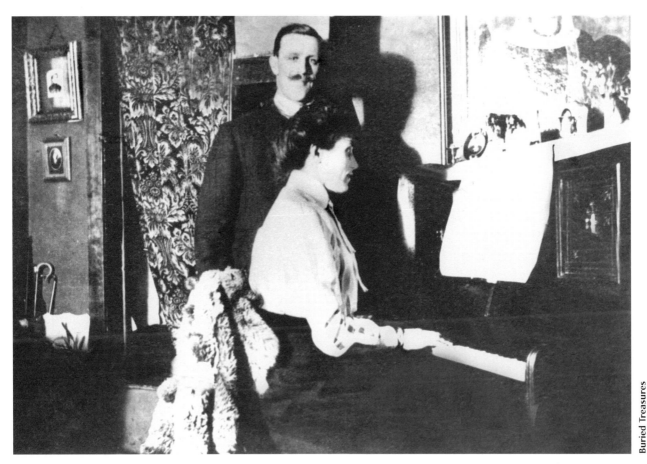

Buried Treasures

Figure 43 – Ralph and Nellie Hogg, Elnora, ca. 1910.

A piano or a reed organ in the parlor was a common indicator of status, as well as a source of solace and pleasure; after the violin, it was the most common instrument on the plains and was brought west in astonishing numbers. Roy "Pappy" Watts, who was later a celebrated member of the CFCN Old Timers (his photo appears on pages 97 and 98) and a bandleader himself, remembered looking in neighbours' windows in suburban Calgary during the early decades of the century: "If they didn't have a piano, you didn't think much of 'em." There are many photographs that demonstrate the role of the piano in a well-appointed home, the sort of home to which many, if not most, aspired.

Although many people can play the piano or organ by ear, these instruments encouraged the reading of music; keyboards come with built-in music holders, after all. Pianos and organs were as symbolic of education, modernity, and technology in the first half of the century as synthesizers and other computer-derived instruments are today.

NC 54-2085

Figure 44 – Crowsnest area, ca. 1930.

Figure 45 – John Holsworth's cabin, Benalto area, ca. 1906.

Figure 46 – Social Club, Pincher Creek, 1895.

NA 2220-6

Figure 47 — Bergen, ca. 1918.

NA 3731-10

Figure 48 — Calgary, early 1900s.

Dad drove the team of horses and the wagon all the way to Trochu to buy a second hand piano for me for my birthday. It was a cabinet grand, and it was the most wonderful thing I had ever seen. And to add to the excitement, Mrs. Stacel agreed to give me piano lessons. She loved music so much, and she passed that love on to me. I would like to say that I went on to be a famous concert pianist, but of course I didn't. But to this day I play the same piano, softly and with feeling, the way I was taught by Mrs. Stacel. Adele Templeton, **Our Huxley Heritage**.

Mother and Dad both enjoyed music. As a result, we had a variety of musical instruments in our home. The big moment came when the piano arrived from the East. This big purchase was made on the instalment plan just prior to the hungry thirties. Dad used to have Anne write letters to the company promising payment as soon as the pigs were sold. Those Easterners must have thought pigs took a awfully long time to mature in the West but eventually the last payment was made and the piano was ours. Regardless of the hard times we had many good times. Our house was a gathering place for young people for singsongs, games and dancing. Mary Johnson, **Wheatfields and Wildflowers**.

Historian Paul Voisey has revised the notion that pioneers were "too busy making a living" to have time for culture: "Farming, of course, is a seasonal activity, but grain-growing in western Canada became one of the most seasonal agricultural systems in the world.... Once the fallow lay cultivated and the crop still awaited the binder, farmers could steal away for hours, or even for days at a stretch" (158). Many of those "stolen" hours were spent in cultural and social activities. Music came to Alberta with the earliest immigrants, as it had with the Native people who settled Canada thousands of years earlier. We should not think of it as a luxury or an indulgence that comes after prosperity.

In the great parlor of the house of the Hudson's Bay factor is a piano, an instrument the like of which is not in Canada. A hundred or more years ago it was manufactured in England by John Broadwood and Co., of English oak and steel. When new it was shipped to Canada to a Hudson's Bay factor, unloaded at Hudson's Bay, and taken to some far post. Twenty years ago Mr. Wilson purchased it in Winnipeg, and then brought it with him across the cold seven hundred miles of winter trail from Edmonton to Fort Vermilion, when he came to take charge of the post. L.V. Kelly, **North With Peace River Jim**.

Nearly in every home, there was someone who could play some instrument, even if it was a harmonica. A.T. Bisgrove, **Wagon Trails Grown Over**.

The important thing is that during the worst depression in modern history, through drought, grasshoppers and the lean years, culture did not die in our small town. Through the drama group, the concert orchestra, and the annual music festival, it flourished and brought a taste of better things to our lives. Harry Carrigan, **Where the Prairie Meets the Hills**.

Not only did they play music, they also made instruments and Albertans have always sought out music teachers.

Figure 49 – H.L. Geis with violins he made, Barrhead, early 1900s.

The Golden Years

NA 4727-2

Figure 50 — George Narolsky, Lamont, ca. 1935.

OB3966

Figure 51 — A violin lesson at College Saint-Jean, Edmonton, in 1948.

NA 3057-1

Figure 52 — Professor Lucien C. Augade, violinist, teacher, and bandleader. His son Louis also figured significantly in music in Calgary in the first half of the twentieth century.

ND-3-2863

Figure 53 — This shot of Mrs. Hales (at the centre of the composition) and her students from Alberta College in Edmonton was taken at McDougall Church, Edmonton, May 1925, perhaps on the occasion of a recital at the church. Many of these students possessed instruments that some present-day musicians would envy. Mrs. Hales's five-string banjo, several of the mandolins, and the rare mandolin-banjos are especially enticing!

ND 2-188

Figure 54 — String teacher and class, Lacombe, undated.

ND 2-266

Figure 55

ND 2-267

Figure 56

ND 2-268

**Figure 57 — A busy teacher, Mr. Hopkins, and three different classes
from a couple of decades later in Lacombe. The extent of this teacher's
influence can be inferred from the number of his students.**

It shouldn't be surprising that by the 1920s, Calgary could fill a large arena, the Stampede Corral, for an operatic recital (Fig. 58).

The large and honored symphony orchestras of today have deeper roots in the province than one may suspect. While generally such aggregations, like the larger brass bands and more complex theatrical performances, occurred in urban centers or where mines brought together large groups of people (many of them coming from such European areas as Wales, where orchestral and choral performance had an extensive history), this was not always the case.

The Laschinsky family came to the Entwhistle region in 1922. "We joined the dance orchestra formed by Dave Lamont, who was a fireboss in the mine.... As we had trained in classical music, it was hard to switch to jazz. My sister also formed a small orchestra for classical music.... They met weekly, and added to the cultural side of the community". Annie Graham, **Foley Trail Vol.II***.*

MADAM GALLI CURCI RECITAL
UNDER THE AUSPICES OF
CALGARY WOMEN'S MUSICAL ASSOCIATION.
OCT 16 1926.

FLASH REEVES & YOUNG

NA 4019-9

Figure 58

A Barn Dance was held at St. Barnabas Hospital, Onoway, during the summer, 1916, when the barn loft was empty of hay. The loft had no stairway and was normally reached by a vertical ladder. I think a temporary stairway was installed, and the whole barn was well cleaned and washed. People came for miles, and the loft was well-filled with happy people. There was no drunkeness or rowdyism. Miss Storrar presided with the help of some of the gentlemen. Coffee was brewed on a stove outside in a washboiler, and ladies brought sandwiches and cakes....

Music was provided by the Cook brothers from Glenford. One of them was Dick, a slim nine-year-old who already bore the stamp of genius which later led him to a life of very successful violin playing and teaching at Alberta College. This barn dance was perhaps his first appearance before an audience, many of whom knew music and were astonished at the boy's rendering of both popular and classical selections he performed so well. Dick was helped by his family to take lessons, including a course from Leopold Auer in Chicago, and his progress was spectacular. Percy Moore, **The Pathfinders**.

NA 4962-1

Figure 59 — A small orchestra in Calgary, 1891.

NA 2039-1

Figure 60 — Calgary Symphony Orchestra, 1913.

Figure 61 – August 1926.

Figure 62 – A Crowsnest area orchestra rehearsing in the Knights of Columbus Hall, Blairmore, ca. 1942.

Crowsnest Pass:
A Miniature World in Alberta
Preserved by Thomas Gushul

NC 54-2075

Figure 63

Gushul had been an avid violinist in his youth despite the ardent objections of his mother, who considered musicians a disreputable lot. Nonetheless, along with a group of village musicians, he gave a command performance for the King and Queen of Romania. His love of music was reflected in his constant support of the annual Crowsnest Pass Music Festival, the Crowsnest Symphony Orchestra, and other local performers. Dave Henry, "Biographical Sketch."

NA 4279-6

Figure 64 – Nick Nahorniak, tsymbaly, Thomas Gushul, violin, East Coleman, 1917–18.

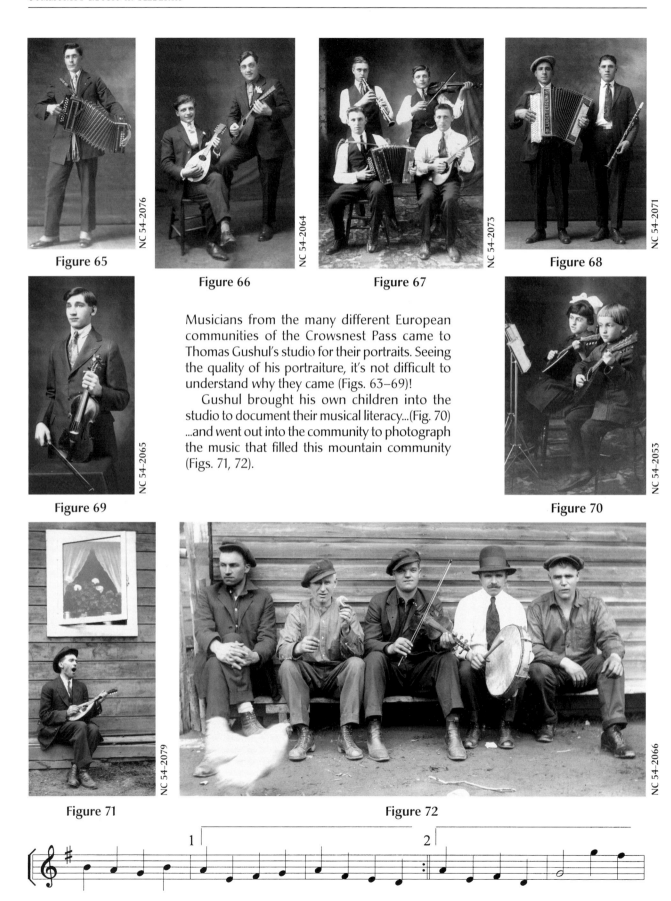

Figure 65

NC 54-2076

Figure 66

NC 54-2064

Figure 67

NC 54-2073

Figure 68

NC 54-2071

Figure 69

NC 54-2065

Musicians from the many different European communities of the Crowsnest Pass came to Thomas Gushul's studio for their portraits. Seeing the quality of his portraiture, it's not difficult to understand why they came (Figs. 63–69)!

Gushul brought his own children into the studio to document their musical literacy...(Fig. 70) ...and went out into the community to photograph the music that filled this mountain community (Figs. 71, 72).

Figure 70

NC 54-2053

Figure 71

NC 54-2079

Figure 72

NC 54-2066

The voice is the first instrument...

The voice is the first instrument. The psalmist who commands us to make that joyful noise expects that we will *sing* our praise. So the congregation sings, as well as it listens to the rehearsed presentation of the choir. The ambitious, of course, may always join the choir and thereby gain some musical instruction.

Some Albertans gathered for hymn singing at hours we now reserve for more secular activities (Fig. 75).

Figure 73 — First Baptist Church Choir, Calgary, ca. 1943.

Figure 74 — Sts. Peter and Paul choir, Mundare, 1946.

Figure 75 – Calmar, 1913.

Figure 76 – Male Quartette, Calgary, ca. 1931.

Memories of Mundare

Figure 77 — High School choir, Mundare, with a trophy they won.

NA 5093-45

Figure 78 — CBC Excelsior Glee Club performing on CFAC, Calgary, 1954.

G2524

Figure 79 — Taras Schevchenko Concert, April 5, 1959.

*All week we looked forward to our Sunday night 'sing-song.' After supper we would go to the church and sing hymns and sacred songs in the gathering twilight. Mother played the organ, our guests went, too, and there were always some, for a bachelor's life was lonely and Sunday was his visiting day.... People from the closer farms dropped in too, and we had a merry time. I think the adults thought of their old homes as they sang the familiar hymns. Lillian B. Robinson, **Vermilion Memories**.*

Others preferred secular songs (or combined programs), solo or in groups of various sizes.

*Mrs. Paul Flint had trained her children to sing harmony, and the three sang at most entertainments — in duets, quartettes, Gilbert and Sullivan Operettas, Minstrel Shows, or whatever was called for. 'I always got so nervous before it was time to sing that I would have to go outside and "flip my biscuits,"' Effie confessed. Beth Sheehan, **Beaverlodge to the Rockies**.*

Keeping The Traditions Alive

Figure 80 – An afternoon at the Shandro Museum, a Ukrainian cultural conservatory near Edmonton, in 1966.

While the "melting pot" theory of North American culture claimed that many of the devices of older worlds would disappear on our brave new continent, this has clearly not happened. These photos demonstrate a few of the ways in which the past has been maintained as part of the culture of the present and future.

Two Ukrainian zithers: the *tsymbaly* and the somewhat more rare *bandura*.

One of the most common dance ensembles in Ukraine historically consisted of a violin lead with the accompaniment of the tsymbaly and a frame drum known as the *bubon*. The technique of performing upon this drum, which resembles both a tamborine and one sort of hand drum used by Native people, is somewhat similar to that used on the Irish *bodhran*: rather than simply beat out the underlying rhythm of a piece, as we generally expect a bass drum to do, the drummer approximates the pattern of the melody. (See Fig. 72 for a picture of this sort of drum; the washtub in Fig. 164 may have been used similarly.)

The tsymbaly, also known as the hammered dulcimer, seems to have originated in Persia, from which it spread across the world. An ancestor of the piano, the dulcimer (as its name implies) produces a sweet, ringing sound, though in the hands of a rhythm-loving hammerer, it can offer fiery music, indeed. In dance ensembles, the tsymbaly had primarily a rhythmic function. As young immigrants began to develop their taste for jazz, it was logical to replace the tsymbaly with another stringed timekeeper, the tenor banjo. A good bubonist could adapt to a full drumkit, and the violinist might switch to hot trumpet or saxophone, and voilà! *Ukrainian Jazz!* (See Fig. 191 and Fig. 192 for ensembles of this type; the latter still includes a tsymbaly in its lineup.)

Figure 81 – Peter Szachio, bandurist, 1976.

Figure 82 – June 1, 1988.

Figure 83 – June 1, 1988.

Musicians and dancers at a Wednesday afternoon session at Calgary's Kerby Centre, 1988. Some of the range of their repertoire can be seen as we read over the pianist's shoulder. (Fig. 82–84)

Figure 84 – June 1, 1988.

Figure 85 – Ben Crane and Rob Holland are active participants in the cowboy poetry revival, singing older songs from the cowboy tradition and writing new songs and encouraging others to do the same. Crane is highly regarded for his multi-instrumental skills and Holland for his rich, warm baritone.

Figure 86 – David Wilkie, shown here with guitarist Nathan Tinkham accompanying Wilf Carter at the Calgary Folk Festival in 1989, is a progressive country musician who appreciates the complex roots of his music. With Tinkham and Cindy Church, Wilkie created the Great Western Orchestra, playing on the name of western Canada's most famous brand of blue jeans, but also referring to the prairie use of the term "orchestra" to denote a combo which performed for dances.

Figure 87 – Olds, 1940s.

Figure 88 – Shandro Museum, 1966.

Young people sometimes return to the older traditions (Figs. 85, 86).

Children are often led to older traditions by their families, who wish to maintain their heritage. A degree of bewilderment, either at the mixture of past and present or due merely to the tension of performance, can sometimes be seen in the young people's faces (Figs. 87, 88).

But when they keep up their involvement, as many do, the results of their dedication can be spectacular (Fig. 89).

Of course, older traditions are altered by the processes of preservation. The song list on the piano at the Kerby Centre includes tunes from the fifties and sixties as well as from earlier decades; one hears of country dances where the band swings from a polka to Bruce Springsteen's latest hit! The Scottish and Ukrainian dancers in these photos recreate on stages, for passive audiences, dances which in many cases were participatory in their homelands.

Figure 89 – Ukrainian Cultural Heritage Village, August 29, 1977.

"Band" invariably meant "brass band"...

In western Canada, the word "orchestra" historically referred to an ensemble which provided music for dancing; it might be as small as one violin and one accompanying instrument (a piano was usually preferred). "Band" invariably meant "brass band." Orchestras were relatively informal and commonplace, though, as we shall see, they became formalized, even professional, before long. Bands, which required skills and equipment not so commonplace, could not be created without a certain amount of planning, but many Alberta communities considered the creation and maintenance of a brass band essential for picnics, ceremonies, and parades.

In 1910 a group of Barons businessmen and farmers formed the Barons Band Syndicate. They sold shares in this to buy band instruments....They also collared citizens and

Figure 90 – Foremost City Band, late 1910s (notice the boy holding the music for the cornetist/leader).

Figure 91 – A band concert near Bowden, ca. 1917. The bandstand appears to be separated from the grandstand by a race concourse, which must have made it difficult to hear any pianissimo passages. The banner on the bandstand advertises the Fair Dance.

Figure 92 – Heather Brae Band, Ferry Point, undated.

Figure 93 – Blairmore, 1927.

41

Figure 94

Figure 95 – Lethbridge Miners Band, ca. 1912.

Figure 96 — The brass band of the 10th Battalion, Calgary Highlanders, was founded in 1914; it went overseas with the Battalion and was disbanded after World War I. The band was recreated during the 1920s, but reorganized as a pipe band during the next decade.

persuaded them to contribute to this important community effort; a couple of men collected $1350.00 one day on Main Street. Before they began, only two people in town had had any band experience. **Wheat Heart of the West.**

Albert Paull worked in the mine during the thirties and suspected that he'd gotten his job because of his ability to play the alto sax. The mine's band had twenty-five members, of whom about ten were "subsidized wholly by

the mine." The rest were mineworkers; when a practice was called, miners informed their shift bosses and went to the rehearsal, not the pit. "When McMillan called an orchestra practice you attended." Toni Ross, **Oh! The Coal Branch.**

Although not all bands have regimental connections, military history is an important aspect of the heritage of the brass band. Even today, many Albertans join the reserves in order to participate in a band.

Figure 97 – The Elks Concert Band developed in 1921 from the Calgary Citizens Band; it was disbanded approximately twenty years later. The Calgary Citizens Band was created by A.L. Augade in 1903.

In addition to the military, there are various institutions which may support bands. Such an association may be essential, given the expenses involved in maintaining a band: instrument purchase and repair, music, possibly instruction, uniforms, and storage space. It was (and is) not uncommon for bandleaders to receive a fee for their expertise. This practice has helped draw musicians to the province (to rural districts as well as to the cities), making them available for private instruction and as providers of dance music.

Perhaps the most significant of these associations is the Salvation Army (Figs. 98–100).

Figure 98 – First Salvation Army Band in Calgary, 1892.

Figure 99 – Cornerstone Ceremony, Salvation Army Barracks, Calgary, 1909.

Figure 100 – Salvation Army Citadel Band, Edmonton, 1920.

Figure 101 — Endiang Band, 1929. The presence of a female cornetist in this band is a bit of a surprise.

Figure 102 — For the Crossfield Band, ca. 1905, individual suit jackets and matching band caps were sufficient to designate band membership.

Figure 103 – Sometimes co-ordinated street clothing served as uniforms. Lacombe Band, 1935.

Figure 104 – Sometimes uniforms evoked the local heritage as well as the military connection.
15th Alberta Light Horse Band, early 1900s.

Band uniforms ranged from nonexistent to practical to elaborate (and sometimes to the silly!). But always, membership in a band was source of pride and prestige (Figs. 105–107).

Where there are brass bands, there are parades, formal and informal, marking events of national, commercial, or political significance (Figs. 108–112).

Figure 106

Figure 105 – Pipemaster Auld of the Calgary Highlanders.

Figure 107 – ca. 1894.

Figure 108 – Calgary Citizens Band marching, possibly on 17th Avenue SW, 1910s.

Figure 111 – A young band sponsored by the Legion leads a pararde to open the Gleichen town fair in August 1987.

Figure 109 – May Day Demonstration, Blairmore, 1930.

Figure 112 – Calgary Stampede Parade, July 1951.

Figure 110 – Modern Woodmen of America, Lacombe, undated.

A specialized variety of regimental band includes only bagpipes and drums.

Bagpipes have a complicated history, in and away from Scotland. Their well-known role in military bands, massed in ranks with swirling bass drumsticks and tightly tuned snaredrums, is relatively recent. In ancient days and in many lands, they have been used for dances and for solo virtuoso performances. I've seen no evidence that *piobaireachd* (pronounced *pibroch*), the great classical music of the Scottish pipes, flourished in early Alberta, but there have been lovers of pipe music — as well as its detractors! — from the earliest days of European settlement on the prairies. One of the earliest references to music in Calgary notes bagpipe tunes wafting over the fort at twilight.

Figure 113 — A piper and dancers helped to celebrate the opening of a gas station in Calgary, 1950s. The opening of service stations and other sorts of commercial establishments often called for entertainment.

Figure 114 — The pipe band of the First Battalion, Calgary Highlanders standing for a portrait...

Figure 115 – ...and emerging from Mewata Armory. Calgary, 1950s.

NA 2362-31

Figure 116 – Pipers like to pace while they play, even when they're not marching. Lockie McMillan used the boardwalk in front of the Alberta Hotel in Crossfield for stage, ca. 1910.

NC 29-15

Figure 117 – An unknown piper entertained at the outdoor cribbage finals in Thorsby in April 1931.

NA 3736-9

NC 54-4389

Figure 118 – A piper led this May Day parade in Blairmore, 1932, to support workers' rights.

Trails, Trials and Triumphs

Figure 119 – The Daysland Pipe Band helped Robert Cowie to celebrate his birthday.

NA 4705-6

Figure 120

Band training can also be used to produce nonmilitary music, as well, a service Albertans have always been pleased to have available. Here a grouping of Army bandmembers perform in uniform for a dance at the Varsity Hall in Sylvan Lake, ca. 1941 (Fig. 120).

Fiddle Contests and Fiddle Culture

Figure 121 – Warming up. Elmer and Ralphene Bolinger in their RV at the Seventh Annual Grand North American Old Time Fiddle Championship held at the Red Barn, a dance hall north of Edmonton, in 1987. The Bolingers travelled throughout western North America, entering contests. Elmer, who died in early 1995, frequently won in the Seniors category. Ralphene, a sensitive accompanist, contributed in no small measure to his success. They kept an electronic keyboard in the RV for practice.

The fiddle remains at the heart of old time music in Alberta. Since the late sixties, fiddle contests and jamborees have proliferated throughout the province. These are often held in conjunction with a fair. A jamboree is structured no differently from a

Figure 123

Figure 124 – Gleichen, September 29, 1990. One fiddler warms up and another rosins his bow, while both wait for the show to begin.

Figure 122 – October 1, 1988. It's not uncommon for wives and husbands to play together, though it is revealing that men most often take the lead while women accompany them. A couple get ready to go on at Gleichen in 1988; note the woman's overhand approach to the fretboard – she's actually using a steel bar, in the Hawaiian style.

Figure 125 — High River Fiddle Contest, August 22, 1987. This event coincided with the town fair; a flatbed trailer was driven into the agricultural arena to serve as the contest stage.

Figure 126

Figure 127 — High River, 1987. Fiddlers re-establish old acquaintances, make new ones, and joke away their tensions as the hall fills and the sound system is set up and checked out. Sometimes backstage joshing fulfills a tactical purpose, creating various forms of psychological pressure before the contest itself actually begins. Note the trophies awaiting the winners on the stage.

Figure 128 — October 1, 1988. Roy Logan, assisted by Ralphene Bolinger at the piano, won another round at Gleichen in 1988. Logan drew upon over thirty years of continuous experience at dance band playing and could boast of dozens of trophies for his fiddling. I heard stories of players who wouldn't bother to attend a contest if they believed that Logan would appear.

Figure 129 — October 1, 1988. This contestant shows in his face the emotion that good old time fiddling can produce, reminding us of the "fine sweet music" which helped Mary Turner give birth happily in 1912.

contest; each player performs two or three tunes, but no prize is awarded. All contests and some jamborees require that the pieces be selected from specific categories: the reel, jig, and waltz.

At some jamborees, everyone gets a trophy, including one for the fiddler who's driven farthest to attend! Prizes at fiddle contests may be only ribbons or trophies, but they sometimes range into hundreds of dollars. Sometimes the awards are planned so that every player gets one!

Figure 130 – Like jamborees, contests typically end with a jam session at which everyone plays together, so the unifying function of music is reinforced. Here's the closing session at Gleichen in September 1990.

Figure 131 – Olds Fiddle Jamboree, August 6, 1987. Whether the events and prize money are large, small, or nonexistent, the audiences for fiddle music remain devoted. Fiddle events may not fill the Saddledome or either of the Jubilee Auditoria, but the music attracts all ages and shows no sign of dying out...

Figure 132 – ...how could it, when young fiddlers like this chap at the Olds Jamboree, are as thrilled to hear other fiddlers as they are to show off their own skills? Olds, 1987.

Any account of music must consider dancing...

ny account of music must consider dancing; for many people, dancing is what makes music essential.

Dad played for many dances and house parties.... He seldom accepted money for himself for this. Dad had been a band leader of the Markerville Brass Band in southern Alberta. He played the cornet. He also played the violin.... The first instrument, other than what Dad had, in our home was a tenor banjo. Brother Peter saved dimes until he had enough for a secondhand banjo. The next was a guitar which Mom and Dad bought at Ben and Jean Thate's auction sales. We taught ourselves to play these instruments with some help from Dad. Dad learned to play violin from a correspondence course. He'd also learned how to read music. It was a real honor for me to go to a dance with Dad, and then to be able to help play for the dance, too. I learned to chord on the banjo and guitar....

While I was accompanying Dad on the guitar, I would get so intent on watching the people dance that my timing would slow down. Dad would either shout or poke me, and with the tap of his toe or nods of his head he'd get me back in time....

One of our teachers taught us to dance as part of P.E. We'd learned most of the basic dances when one of the parents put a stop to it. They said we were going to school to learn, not to play. Even though I knew how to dance

I was too shy to accept a dance from the opposite sex. Then one night at a Blue Hill School dance, my dad turned the fiddle over to someone else and came over to me and said, 'Ella, it's time you got out and danced.' He was the first gentleman that I danced with. Ella Bjornson Thate, **Where Friends and Rivers Meet**.

Solo dance traditions, such as stepdancing, allow people to express their musical spirits, at nearly any time or place (Fig. 133).

Pete McDougal was a fun lover and enjoyed games and dancing. At a party at the Boyd Perkins house, someone chorded on the piano while Pete did a jig. The idea was that the pianist picked a spot on the floor with her eye and the closer Pete came to the spot, she

Figure 133 — Black Diamond, 1890s.

NA 5403-2

Figure 135 – Jack Blachly's band at a dance at Bowness Park, Calgary, ca. 1938.

NC 54-277

Figure 134 – Crowsnest area, ca. 1915.

*raised the key. I can still remember how the whole house shook. Ethel Rollag, **Homestead Country**.*

*Dad loved music, and when we'd wind up the gramophone he would step dance for us until, on several occasions, the stove pipes fell down. What a sooty mess that created! Mina Noble, **A Century of Memories**.*

In addition to schools, barns, church halls, hotels, and community halls, Albertans liked to build *boweries* on which to dance. A bowery might be merely an outdoor dance floor (Fig. 134), but it was often elaborately covered with greenery, to become a truly Edenic bower (Fig. 135).

The Staveley dance pavilion was erected in 1926, "...with a covered orchestra stand together with a refreshment stand. They agreed to turn over a percentage of their profits to the Willow Creek Club for improvement of the ground. These dances were of the jitney-type, ten cents per dance or three for a quarter. At the end of each dance, the floor

NA 2923-5

Figure 136 — The bowery dance began as simply an outdoor dance, which some people still find attractive. Beaverlodge during the thirties; note the fiddler seated at the right.

was cleared with a big rope and everyone paid to get back on the floor.... One night Len Davis brought a black singer with a beautiful baritone voice and his rendition of 'When the Moon Comes Over the Mountain' brought him repeated encores from the crowd delirious with happiness under the huge golden prairie moon." Glenn Stanford, **The Butte Stands Guard**.

Bowery dances were only held in the summer. The men would build a plank floor. Then everyone would go to the bush to gather aspens. They cut down the ones about ten feet tall. They were fastened at the bottom and allowed to drape over towards the centre of the floor. That evening the dance would be in full swing with local talent providing the music. **Lanterns on the Prairie**.

It was not uncommon at winter weddings, for that seemed to be the generally accepted and convenient time from work for such bliss, to see guests dancing outdoors in the cold on a wooden platform built for the occasion. Usually the violin and dulcimer were the only instruments that would take the punishing temperature, which nevertheless added zest to the dance, which we five and six-year olds (this was over sixty years ago) ogled in awe at the joy and performances of the dancers. I do recall seeing Dad 'fiddling' the violin with woolen gloves from which the fingers of the left hand were removed so that he could finger the notes. William Chahley, **Our Legacy**.

Eventually, community boosters and other entrepreneurs created dance halls, often in pleasant rural locations which might attract young pleasure seekers from the city as well as the country- side (Fig. 137).

Some structures were temporary. "With so many families among the settlers, the need for a school soon became apparent. Fairdale, Westdale, and Highland Park School districts were all formed that fall, 1911. That winter they had the lumber all piled up to build Highland Park School when some of the young fellows decided there should be a dance, though there was no place to dance. Leonard Jacobson had a little shack near the Johnny Jones place, so he went to the trustees and asked if the lumber could be used for a dance hall. They gave their consent, so they loaded up the lumber and built the 'hall' tight up

Figure 137 – The dance hall at Seba Beach, 1933.

Figure 138 – Members of a dance band that played at Seba Beach during the 1930s.

Figure 139 – Cold Lake, 1930.

Figure 140 – Peace River, 1938.

*against his shack. The roof was flat and the floor just tacked down. A stove was put in, and they had the dance that night. Everybody and his wife was there, and all had a wonderful time. Lester Huston and Lawrence Patterson supplied the music and the caller was up from Sounding Creek. Jack Davies was the master of ceremonies and instigator of the whole affair. After the dance, the lumber was all moved back to the schoolground." **Sibbald Community History**.*

If any evidence is needed to demonstrate that Albertans were always devoted to culture, consider their commitment to the community dance. Getting to and from dances could be difficult. Without a moon there would be no light, and because the roads were uncertain, dances frequently continued all night; people left for home only with the dawn.

Although riding in a sleigh under a buffalo robe, with hot bricks at your feet and the bells a-jingling, fulfills a romantic image of winter travel in Canada, transporting a family or merely crossing a well-known (and consequently boring) tract of land in below zero weather was neither exotic nor romantic. Above are two covered sleighs created by imaginative people who had to get out of the house. Warm, they probably were. Claustrophobic? Undoubtedly. I once read an account of some men who travelled to town in one, with the fire well stoked, drinking whiskey and smoking cigars all the way — a trip I think I'd avoid (Figs. 139–140)!

In those days I loved to dance and one night when my husband had gone to Creston to do some logging with some of the other men, I walked four and a half miles home from a dance in town with a piece of two by four in

*my hand in case I met a coyote. It was 58 degrees below and the northern lights were out and the coyotes were howling. It was a glorious night and I have never forgotten it. Margaret Bernon Martin, **Silver Sage Bow Island 1900-1920**.*

*People travelled mostly by team or horseback those early days. It was nothing to have six or eight couples arrive at a school dance in a sleigh, even with weather below zero. A few inches of hay, several blankets and your favorite partner was very exciting, especially if the trip lasted an hour or so each way. The Letcher Family, **Candlelight Years**.*

*One dance I remember was held in Haakon's barn. The mud was so sticky and deep that a hayrack went from house to house collecting dancers. Margaret Wilson, **Spurs and Shovels Along the Royal Line**.*

My love for music caused [me to endure] many hardships getting to and from dances. We had to go many miles in all types of weather and road conditions. Transportation was by sleigh, horseback, buggy, walking, and in later years by car. I recall leaving home in mid afternoon, early in Spring, to play for a dance at Hand Hills Club House, twenty miles from home. Just after midnight a blizzard blew in, and the president ordered no one to leave, and bargained with us to continue playing. We entertained the folks until six in the morning, then shared a bit of lunch that was left from midnight, and tried to rest in corners and on benches. A few hours later, the storm subsided

Foley Trail Vol. II

Figure 141 – This housewarming party was held near Entwhistle during the early months of World War I. The fiddler was Alec McDairmaid. A newly finished, unfurnished house was an ideal site for a dance. It would be warmer than a barn; indeed, a roomful of dancers, even with no heater, might quickly need to open a window on a cold January night! At least one old timer spoke of a housewarming dance as an easy and pleasant way to smooth a newly laid floor. What role in the entertainment the coyote played is not clear; it appears to be stuffed, although the original caption said it was "frozen."

a bit, and we started out on our long cold journey home. The horses had eaten all the hay out of the box, and all that remained to sit on was a few Russian thistles. The horses found it hard to cope with the cold wind at 37 degrees below 0. On our arrival home, we realized that we had been away for twenty-four hours. Roy Embree, **Hanna North**.

Every time a new settler came they would build a barn and hold a dance in the hayloft to

celebrate.... The ladies would take refreshments, and at midnight we would stop and eat, then dance until three in the morning. John and Anna Bradley would dance the Cakewalk at midnight. They dressed up for this, and that was my introduction to a gentleman in a tuxedo. Tressa Averill Harrington Baxter, **Red Willow Reflections**.

Dances, no matter how frequent, are special occasions — romantic occasions — occasions for intense experience. Photographs, evocative though they may be, only hint at what these couples from the middle of our century were experiencing.

The musicians played waltzes, foxtrots, polkas, one steps, &c. After an interval of dancing, the musicians rested, and then the partners promenaded slowly around the hall until the music started again.

The dance always started with a waltz, and the young men who gathered in a bunch near the door would walk boldly out and choose one of the girls who were sitting demurely on benches around the wall. If the girl accepted the first dance, custom ruled that she was his partner for the evening. She could dance with whoever asked her for the rest of the evening, but she must save the supper waltz for him, and the last dance, after which he would gallantly walk her to her home and then walk the long distance alone to his home. Usually he arrived just in time for his father to thrust a milk pail into his hand to start the day's labors. Being up all night dancing didn't give you license to sleep all day. **Memories Past to Present**.

Mamma and Daddy decided that I could come with Daddy to my first grown-up party, which was to be held at the Garbutt home that night. So, wearing my beautiful organdy dress (from Eaton's), we left Mamma behind with my little brothers and walked back the one-

Figure 142 – A square dance at Bragg Creek, probably during the forties.

Figure 143 – Veteran's Affairs Dance, December 20, 1945.

Figure 144 – MacDonald Hotel, December 12, 1945.

Figure 145

Figure 146 – Orderlies dancing at Mewburn Veterans Hospital, December 3, 1945.

Figure 147 – Dance at Mewburn Hospital, December 6, 1945.

half mile dusty road, through evening shadows, carrying our trusty coal-oil lantern; fireflies danced and the river murmured softly as we climbed the river bank. Yellow lighted windows and jolly voices mixed with oldtime fiddle and mouth organ music reached us. The rooms were full of people of all ages. Some young men had brought girls by team and buggy from the district west of us. I watched from the bedroom door as the pretty young 'flappers' giggled and smoothed down the sleek 'bobs' of their hair or heated the curling iron to touch up a windblown 'spit-curl'. One dark and attractive girl always glows in my memory. She wore a scarlet crepe formal, ruffled around her ankles and with a sash tied

Ks502/2

Figure 148 — Vermilion, November 1953.

in the back. Our 1970 fashions are very similar.

Some couples played whist while others stood waiting to dance to our local musicians. Somehow, one of my girl friends persuaded her older brother to ask me to dance. I was twelve years old at the time, and this was the first time I had ever danced at a house party. I could hardly believe it, as I shyly stumbled around! What a patient and polite boy he was! How was I to know what fun we'd all have in four or five years, dancing at our local Gilby Hall, **Homesteads and Happiness***.*

The girls [new immigrants from England] were gay and high spirited, and we loved to

watch them dance. One night at Ottawa school, they were in a quadrille where the men linked left arms in the centre, put their rights arms about their partners' waists and whirled about in a pinwheel at great speed, sometimes sweeping the girls off their feet. In the midst of this, a sleeping dog rose from the corner and slunk towards the door. The group Olive was in was whirling madly when the dog crossed her path. She leaped into the air and was swept over his back, landing like thistledown beyond him. She carried on blithely as if this were a part of the dance. Not so the dog. He gave a yelp of terror and fled. Lillian B. Robinson, **Vermilion Memories***.*

Figure 149 – Ukrainian Catholic Church carnival, Radway, August 8, 1964.

Figure 150 – The Owl Dance in progress at a Siksika Christmas celebration, Gleichen, ca. 1947. The Owl Dance is one of the few couple dances typically encountered at Pow Wows.

Figure 151

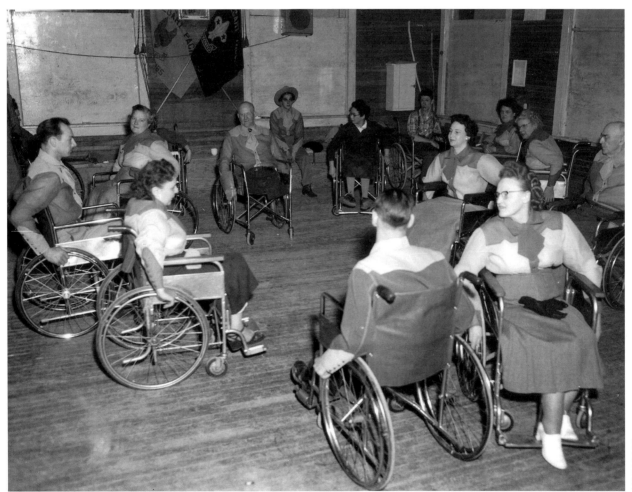

Figure 152 – Calgary, 1955.

Figure 153 – Stampede during the 1930s.

Figure 154 – 1952.

Figure 155 – Stampede square dancing in front of the new city hall, July 9, 1988.

Figure 156 – Harold Anderson, Stampede Week, 1989. The heart of Stampede square dancing, held for many years in a roped–off portion of 8th Avenue in front of Eaton's, has been the fiddle music of Harold Anderson. He and the band play through the morning, supporting a variety of callers and dancers.

The dances during the winter were family affairs; everybody danced, even the children. I used to tag the men Mother was dancing with, and they were quite willing to dance with a little girl. Therefore before I was nine years old I knew how to dance all the dances of the time, such as waltzes, polkas, one step, two step and several others, also the quadrilles (square dances, as they are called now). Maemi (Kangas) Scott, **From Hoofprints to Highways***.*

Coal oil lanterns strung amongst the rafters gave an eerie flickering light, so a hasty kiss

or an extra squeeze could pass unnoticed. Mrs. E. Bell, **Beiseker's Golden Heritage***.*

Old time dances — the waltz, polka, and two step — gradually became passé, and new dances, including the Charleston, Fox Trot, Moonlight Waltz, and especially the Bunny Hug ("...which we knew the girls needed most"), came into favor with the young people, though not always their elders. "Couples were stopped on the floor doing numbers which were outlawed, especially the Bunny Hug, so they left the dance for home or some other point ... where dancing as you please was allowed." John Julius Martin, **The Prairie Hub***.*

Of course, romance and passion and all their trappings are prime candidates for parody, as for the disapproval of elders. William Rutledge Gore came to the Kneehill district from England, ca. 1900; he was the master of ceremonies at dances and other events, and was known for his wit, calling out at one dance, "I see we have Irene in her crepe-de-chine, you can see more of Irene than the crepe-de-chine." L.Grace Gore, **M.D. of Kneehill 1904-1967***.*

Sitting Wind enjoys pow-wows and looks forward to them eagerly. He is one of the best chicken dancers and was made champion at Banff Indian Days last summer.

According to Stoney custom any male who wishes to dance with a girl must go and stand by the drummers, his back turned to the females, and wait for a girl to select him. The girls watch to see which boys are making their way to the center. Kathleen must have been watching for him to make his move, because she was right there as soon as he melded into the circle of booming rhythm, her slight finger poking gently into the small of his back. He turned his head, saw her eyes: oblique, questioning. She was even shorter than he, it struck him again; exactly the right height for him. Peter Jonker, **The Song and the Silence: Sitting Wind, The Life of Stoney Indian Chief Frank Kaquitts***.*

69

A2875

Figure 157 — One of the proverbial blind fiddlers, Ross Newell, played for dances in the Stony Plain area. He might have performed by himself, though he probably preferred to have a piano to accompany him. Accompaniment was also sometimes provided by reed organ, which was lighter than a piano, an important feature if it had to be transported across the countryside to or from the schoolhouse. (We can see this event occurring in the delightful NFB film about music and dance in the Drumheller area, **Every Saturday Night**.) Guitar, banjo, ukulele, and autoharp were also used to accompany the fiddler. Accompaniment increased the volume of the music and emphasized the beat for dancers; it was helpful, but not essential. One occasionally reads of dances held with only a harmonica player; if this really happened, the musician would need lungs of leather and the stamina of an ox!

The Battle River Country

Figure 158 — Paul's Orchestra, Battle River, 1910. They were too early to play jazz, and one doesn't expect to find ragtime harp on the Northern Range, so what did they play? Elegant interpretations of Tin Pan Alley hits? Light classical music, such as "Liebestraum" or "Carnival of Venice"? Genteel polkas, schottisches, and waltzes?

Figure 159 — A "novelty" group from Edgerton, 1927. "Novelty" items were light, often jazz-influenced, tunes which we would call "pop." Some novelty songs were trivial, even silly ("The Aba Daba Honeymoon" or "Yes, We Have No Bananas"), but not all of them were. A good jazz blower could make something well worth hearing out of "Bye Bye Blackbird" or "The Sheik of Araby."

Figure 160 — Some of the same musicians from the previous photo, possibly at a later date.

Figure 161 — The Bradbury Orchestra of Edberg, with their teacher, Mr. Wright, in 1924.

Figure 162 — The band at the Hughendon Community Hall, 1926.

The urge to dance sometimes finds expression in unexpected places — on ice (Fig. 150)...and in wheelchairs (Fig. 152).

Calgarians in particular like to dance in the street. At least, some of them do. Although several writers have claimed that this custom is emblematic of the city's western heritage and freewheeling spirit, street dancing generally only happens once a year, during Stampede, and many of the participants are tourists (Figs. 153–156).

An important aspect of the story of dance music in Alberta, as throughout North America, is the growth of African influence through ragtime, jazz, rock and roll, &c. The earliest European dance music in the province was probably provided by the

A14058

Figure 163 – Hines Creek, ca. 1932.

Land of Red and White

Figure 165 – Heinsburg Old Timers, 1940s.

The Big Band

Figure 164 – The wash tub in this combo undoubt-edly served as an adequate bass drum. Dance music sometimes included improvisation and was always lively. It is not surprising that Ukrainians, Czechs, Jews, and other immigrants from Europe took so quickly to hot jazz from the American South; their native musics had much in common with it.

fiddle. While the repertoires of early Alberta fiddlers certainly extended beyond the jigs and reels of Britain, these musicians probably lacked the rhyth-mic swing and playful timbres that later character-ized country fiddling. Such jazzy elements were not initially accepted in all communities.

All ages went to dances. As some of the new dances came out, some of the older people thought they were disgraceful. Idella and her partner were once told to 'sit down or stop ragging.' This turned out to be the one-step. **Harvest of Memories**.

NA 3017-10

Figure 166 – Percy Copithorne, violin, at a dance at Jumping Pound, ca. 1950.

A solo fiddler, or a fiddler with basic accompani-ment, might do for a small dance in a schoolhouse or living room, but as halls grew, and tastes changed, larger ensembles were needed. Here we have a panorama of dance orchestras, whose music — mostly lost to us now — must have ranged widely. Note the visual cues that many of them give of their sophistication. For example, music casually (or not!) left visible demonstrates that the musicians can read it (Fig. 160). Not all do, by the way. As in most regions, quite a few musicians in Alberta never need to learn to read or read only enough that "it doesn't get in the way of my playing," to use a time-honored phrase. Although community music in the province may have often been informal, it would be a mistake to imagine that it was unlearned or simple. Even a self-taught fiddler who doesn't read music will have spent countless hours practising and absorbing music. And there were music teachers throughout Alberta!

Figure 167 — The Roy Logan Orchestra (left to right: Hugh Carlson, Logan, Myrtle Holt, Mildred Logan) at Prince's Island Park August 3, 1987.

On that particular evening, I was dragged from an obscure corner that seemed to fit well with my innate shyness and ordered to play [my fiddle]. Not alone, for there at the piano sat old Frank. He'd been teamstering in the mountains, too, and he was grumpy as an old bear. He said, "Now, just you keep up the beat, don't stop to make corrections and don't apologize, no matter what." Frank would keep the tempo steady by chording on the piano. He did. I did. It was my first experience with that sort of accompaniment. How easy and smooth it became, playing for such an appreciative audience! "They Cut Down The Old Pine Tree," all those changes, then waltzes, squares, schottische, heel and toe polka, mostly numbers I'd learned in Saskatchewan before leaving home, 1931, at age 14, to escape the drought and family conflict.

...But there was more. A very personable young woman insisted upon easing me onto the floor for a lesson in dance. I will always be thankful to Evelyn for helping me overcome that first self-conscious hurdle.

And the people ignored my bumbling shuffle just as politely as they'd ignored the squeaks and squawks from my $7.95 mail order fiddle. Martin Rossander, **A Country Dance 'back in the hills.'**

...sandwiches, cake, and other goodies such as candy and nuts. My mother made the coffee at our house, a half a mile west of the school, in a wash boiler. They then poured it into cream cans, and they came for it about 11:30 p.m., putting blankets over the five gallon cans to keep it as hot as possible. Of course they had to take down the stove in the school and put it in the corner because it got so warm with so many people in the room. After a few dances people got pretty warm, and there were plenty of wilted collars, for that was when

G1965

Figure 168 – Kitchen staff for the Bellis carnival, February 18, 1955.

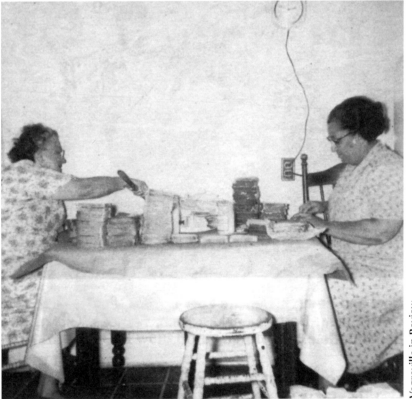

Vegreville in Review

Figure 169 – Alphonsine Benoit and Indianna Paquette made the sandwiches for Emelda Benoit's wedding dance, Vegreville, ca. 1940.

men wore those high stiff collars and nobody ever took off their coats no matter how hot they got. Henry P. Hansen, **Wheat Country**.

By that time happiness was well under way for the dancers, and all of the shy lads and wallflower ladies had been given a whirl on the floor. Some male would announce his appreciation for the fine time being made possible by the musicians. Of course, the women who brought cookies and cakes and sandwiches and made gallons of coffee in the huge copper-bottomed wash boiler worked much harder than any musicians, but that was taken for granted, and so, for the musicians, a collection would be taken. Martin Rossander, "A Musician's Memoir."

Those who provided music for dances were not always paid...

Those who provided music for dances were not always paid and sometimes found their position tedious. No matter how dedicated to music one might be, providing the background for other men to take women in their arms eventually lost its appeal. Gradually various systems of payment were introduced. The most basic involved passing the hat for contributions; even when formal fees or percentages were introduced, the rates were not consistent across the province or the decades. Payment might merely express gratitude and delight and assist a musician in the upkeep of his instrument and repertoire (if he had to purchase sheet music). But it wasn't long before the concept of professionalism took hold throughout the province.

Some fees reported in various local histories:

1900s – $2.00 for dance orchestra.

1930s – Dad Ford's Orchestra played at Styal Hall for $35.00, Entwhistle, June 11, 1937.

– Dewald's Orchestra for $8.00, Entwhistle, June 25, 1937.

– Si Hopkins Orchestra from Calgary was paid ca. $100.00 for playing at dances in rural areas.

– One duet during Depression got $3.00 for a dance.

– Mel Tallon got $3.00 per night in DeBolt.

1940s – $4.50 - 5.00 per night for family orchestra.

– $18.00-19.00 per evening for group.

1961 – $45.00 for band for dance, "less if the turnout was poor."

Rollie Francis, an artist with the violin, travelled far and wide providing music for dances.... The family often said one of the reasons Rollie never married was because he played the violin while others danced with the girls. Edwin Francis, **Times to Remember**.

The local boys that played for the dance were Babe Scar and one of the Welch boys. That was a fiddle and some drums, but Babe Scar said that he thought he could play an accordion, so, sure enough, one of the bush men came through to the bar there a week or so later and he had an accordion with him, and Babe sat in a corner. He'd never seen one before, but he fiddled with it that afternoon and that night he was able to play tunes to please everybody who was in the bar. So Babe said that if we would buy him an accordion he would play for the dances until he paid for it. So we got a raffle going and we sold tickets to the railroad men and some of the conductors took tickets up and down the line. We sold to everybody that went through.... Eventually we sold all the tickets, and we had enough money to buy Babe his accordion. Well, sir, the next dance we had Babe bring that accordion out, and he played us some toe tapping tunes that you couldn't sit through.... I don't know when the accordion was paid for, and I don't believe Babe knows when it was paid for either. Nobody even cared, Babe just played. Mac Peck, **Spirit and Trails of Lac St. Anne**.

I can remember that mother and dad were the only musicians in the area and were much in demand.... When the threshers came to our house at harvest time, the men insisted on washing the dishes and cleaning up the kitchen after their supper, while mother and dad entertained with their music — a Real Night Club.... Any time we were invited to a neighbour's house for the evening, they were expected to entertain. Dad was getting a bit tired of playing, and one time refused to take his violin. Mother put his violin case in the wagon, unknown to him, and proceeded with the family to this neighbour's home. When asked to play, he said that he did not bring the instrument, at which time mother went out to the wagon, picked up the case, and to her embarrassment found that dad had removed the violin. Guess there were some angry words exchanged. Elizabeth (Michelmore) Soper, **Lengthening Shadows of the Neutrals**.

Dad's reputation as a musician did to some extent interfere with his ability to carry on exclusively as a farmer even in those early times. People within the community and the surrounding area, upon learning of his musical ability, made demands on him which he found difficult to refuse. Since Dad had no car and the horses were needed on the farm, he relied almost totally on foot travel to meet his playing engagements. Often because of the distance he would have to walk, he would take his clarinet in its case and would set out on foot a day or two early in order that he might arrive in time for his playing engagement. He played at many Ukrainian weddings in the Delph, Skaro, St. Michael and Lamont areas. These were usually three day affairs and when you added travelling time, it meant that Dad would be away from home a minimum of five days. To make matters worse, his remuneration for his efforts frequently consisted of a chicken or two or maybe a cake, which, by the time he came home, would go stale.

Needless to say, Mother was justifiably unhappy with the situation and by 1932 had persuaded Dad to give up his orchestral involvement. Reluctantly, he agreed, but, so long as he still owned a clarinet, he continued to be plagued by requests and pleas to play for weddings and dances. To permanently resign from further musical involvements, Dad sold his clarinet. I believe it was one of the saddest days of his life, as making music was his first love. Frank Holubowich, **Between River and Lake**.

Wilf Carter got his start in the schoolhouses of the prairies. "We would have the time of our lives, dancing half the night away to a piano or fiddle or whatever the schoolhouse afforded.... Along about 1925 I began to sing at the dances, writing my own songs and entertaining the crowd hour after hour.... The little old schoolhouse would jump with the fun. I look back on those occasions as among the finest of my life. **The Yodelling Cowboy**.

Carter's experience was not unusual. While the band and dancers rested, and everyone had a meal, soloists had the chance to show their stuff. If, like Carter, they were received well, they might be tempted to seek larger audiences on subsequent occasions, perhaps even to develop professional careers. This temptation must have been even more appealing when the neighborhood entertainments graduated from the one room schoolhouse to a hall with a stage and a microphone!

Semi-professional family orchestras proliferated throughout Alberta history, especially in rural locations, where parents and siblings have time to practice together, and even grown and married offspring live nearby. Such families augmented their incomes and shared the pleasures of music and performance. Some of these part-time family groups became fully professional entertainers, occasionally even making their way to vaudeville, Broadway, or radio.

Figure 170 – Smoky Lake, August 21, 1949.

Figure 171 – Sherrill Lanyon of Edmonton performs at the Smoky Lake School Christmas concert, December 21, 1951.

Figure 172 – Amateur Night at H.A. Kostash High School, Smoky Lake, October 4, 1950.

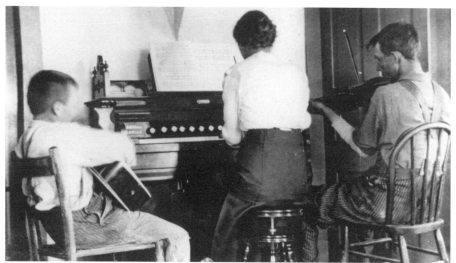

Figure 173 – Andrew, Helma, and Bill Parkkari, Alderson, ca.1916.

NA 2691-16

Figure 174 — Byemoor, 1924: the Babb Family's Whizz Bang Zowie Orchestra. (Before you laugh at the name, consider how silly the ersatz surrealism of band names from the sixties — *Chocolate Watch Band*, say, or *Iron Butterfly* — appears less than half a century later. As a matter of fact, the toughness of some in use as I write may already be recognized as phony: *Anthrax* and *Megadeath*, indeed!) The Babbs's lineup combined old and new elements; to the violin and an old fashioned variety of mandolin, they added a contemporary drum kit and the ever popular Hawaiian guitar.

Leo Bosch came to Water Valley from Russia in 1931. His family orchestra played for dances throughout the area. "When the remaining children were old enough to hang onto an instrument, Leo went to Calgary to buy instruments for all of them and started them playing at a very early age." **Beisker's Golden Heritage**.

Land of Red and White

Figure 175 – The Happy Hortons, Heinsburg, 1948. The Horton family orchestra performed together for about five years, until the children got married and moved away from home. Margaret (Horton) Nelson wrote in 1987, "During the years 1947-1950 we were a very busy orchestra. Our bookings averaged about three engagements per month within a radius of fifty to seventy miles. We always looked forward to a dance and meeting new people."

Figure 176 – The Kozoway brothers, Borden, John, Peter, and Paul, have added the electric lap steel, another form of Hawaiian guitar, to their lineup. Mundare, 1950s.

Memories of Mundare

NA 4950-23

Figure 177 – A Turner Valley band from the late 1930s; at the left in the front sits Ross Alger, who later served briefly as mayor of Calgary.

Gs3/2

Figure 178 – Dance at Mewburn Veterans Hospital, December 6, 1945.

Professionalism in music may begin at school, especially in high school, where young people frequently form dance and performance ensembles of various kinds, sometimes under the guidance of a music teacher. Some groups break up after graduation, but some stay together for years.

Gs11

Figure 179 – Martin Adams Orchestra, May 1, 1946.

Courtesy O. Sveen

Figure 180 – Olaf Sveen entertains tourists in Jasper during the sixties.

NA 4705-9

Figure 181 – Reed section of the pit band, Stampede grandstand, 1977. Stampede functions for Calgary musicians as Christmas does for other businesses: it's a time when money flows. The handsome fellow at bottom right is Eric Friedenberg, whose father Jac came to Alberta from Holland in 1929, having been a professional pianist in Europe for several years. Both father and son have had influential careers as players and teachers in southern Alberta.

NA 4959-1

Figure 182 – Jascha Galprin's orchestra at Lake Louise, 1936. Galprin was an important performer and educator in southern Alberta through the forties; he taught and conducted young people's orchestras at Mount Royal College.

The role of the tourist industry should never be underestimated in any consideration of Alberta culture. Just as rural and suburban areas such as Seba Beach and Fish Creek attracted merrymakers from Edmonton and Calgary, Banff and Jasper have also drawn an international clientele and can be choice locations for professional musicians. Work at these places may not always be either dependable or profitable, but for a lucky few, it is both. For Wilf Carter, a temporary job as the Singing Cowboy accompanying dudes on Banff trail rides led to an international recording career.

A portfolio of professional and semi-professional musicians, urban and rural, from different eras.

NC 54–2080

Figure 183 – Crowsnest area, ca. 1927.

NA 3535–57

Figure 184 – The Nanton Rhythm Aces, early 1930s.

NA 5403-1

Figure 185 — Dance musicians in Calgary, ca. 1930.

A5911

Figure 186 — A Peace River band from the thirties: Bill Duce (Hawaiian guitar) Sam Zwick (violin), Herb Zwick (banjo), Bill Zwick.

Figure 187 – The Sonny Fry Orchestra. Drummer Fry, a resident of Red Deer, formed his group in the late 1930s or early 1940s; they played the Varsity Hall in Sylvan Lake and Penley's Academy in Calgary, among other venues.

Figure 188 – George Lake's Hawaiians, who broadcast over CKUA during the fifties.

Figure 189 – Stu Davis (2nd from right), 1949.
Davis was a country singer whose records are now collectors' items.

Figure 190 – Entertainers at Calgary Stampede Breakfast, 1950.

Figure 191 - Russell Kulchinsky Band, Smoky Lake, April 21, 1955.

Figure 192 – The 5 Gents, March 1956.

Figure 193 – The Rhythm Queens, a smart travelling group from Consort, in 1935. (That town later produced another woman famous in provincial music history, kd lang.) Working in an all-female orchestra undoubtedly saved these women from a number of difficulties they'd have encountered as, say, "girl singer" in an otherwise male travelling group. (The man in the picture was their manager.) Then, as now, the novelty of a stage full of women sold tickets. They must have caused raised eyebrows in some of the smaller towns they visited.

Figure 194 – The young Tommy Banks at the piano during a jam session with Walter "Bones" Eurchuk in the fifties. As throughout the province's history, young Albertans like these were attuned to the musical currents influencing the rest of the continent, in this case cool jazz, bebop, and the blues. After World War Two, communications technology allowed musicians to be in very close touch with these influences. However, despite the sophistication and talent of musicians like Banks, many Albertans, especially the young, continue to fear that the only exciting and valid culture comes from elsewhere.

Figure 195 – Joe Mason stands proudly before his van advertising his services as a One Man Band. Mason plays harmonica (his rack holds five Marine Band models at a time), guitar, drum (bass drum, cymbal, and snare are attached to his right foot), and an eight–note bass (left foot). He most often plays for dances, but the van has a platform at the front where he can set up, and, with his wife at the wheel, he has led not a few parades, and sometimes won a ribbon for the most interesting float!

For many years I managed an orchestra called the 'Nemiskam Serenaders.' Annie Thompson played the piano, Gordon Cowie the piano accordion, Bill Cowie the drums, Bertel (Slim) Eklof the banjo, and I played the trumpet. We had no money to advertise our orchestra on the radio or to purchase bills for distribution, so Ashley Butterwick made posters for us. We didn't buy sheet music in order to learn the new tunes, either. My mother would listen to the radio and when she heard a new tune she would write it down and sing it for me. I played the piano by ear so after she sang the song I would play it and we'd have a new hit tune for the next dance.... We received a small percentage of the 'take' at the door. At 10¢ admission *fee you can see how much we'd get. On looking over our old account book I noticed the most entries brought four or five dollars. The lowest pay we received was $3.00... and the highest was a New Year's dance ...for $12.00 Remember this was the total pay for a five-piece orchestra and these prices were paid as late as 1943-44. Harold Johnson,* **Shortgrass Country**.

Professionalism breeds both versatility and the need to develop images, which might not have much connection to real life. Forest Hale of Evansburg worked in both the western-styled Rocky Mountain Rangers and the more uptown Lorenz Orchestra. Can you spot him in both of these photos (Figs. 196, 197)?

Figure 196 – Rocky Mountain Rangers, May 1937.

Figure 197 – Lorenz Orchestra, undated.

Figure 198 – Notice the strange effect of retouching in this formally posed photo; have different heads been placed on the original players' torsos?

Figure 199 – This postcard photo of Paul Playford's ensemble was made by a more skillful photographer; its composition is as sophisticated as the musicians themselves appear to be. Playford and his group played throughout south/central Alberta. This photograph has appeared in at least two local histories, which is uncommon, so the Orchestra seems to have made an impact upon their audiences.

Figure 200 — Souvenir Christmas card from Mart Kenney, who led the most successful of all western Canadian big bands. The vocalist sprawled seductively here was known as Georgia Dey, but was born in Wetaskiwin as Pearl Collicutt.

As musicians become more professional, they need to advertise. An early form of advertisement, still used in some industries, was the picture post card.

From the Bassano Mail, March 26, 1925: "The Lingenfelter-Walsh Orchestra has broken up. Someone put red pepper in Jake's saxophone and on a great intake he got a mouthful and then he stuck his tongue out at the pianist and asked if it was burned. Of course Walsh thought Jake was making faces at him, and quit on the spot." **Best in the West by a Damsite 1900-1940**.

Some professional musicians from Alberta's past...

Although space does not allow me to recognize all of the noteworthy performers, some professional musicians from Alberta's past are worth particular attention. Readers are invited to honor privately any favorites left out of this collection. (What about Roy Warhurst? Ron Collier? Kathleen Parlow? Hod Pharis?)

Reed player Louis Biamonte led a number of sophisticated dance bands in Edmonton during the thirties, forties, and fifties. Versatility was essential for professional musicians during those years, and in addition to the uptown ensembles we see here, Biamonte also appeared in groups which included the western swing fiddler (of Lebanese parentage) King Ganam and polka maestro Gaby Haas (Figs. 201-204).

Louis Biamonte in The Social Credit Band 1939

A10887

Figure 201

Figure 202 – Edmonton Serenaders, 1946.

Figure 203 – 1948.

BI 1887/1

Gaby Haas came to Canada from Czechoslovakia in 1938. After a few years in Saskatoon, he moved to Edmonton, where he was a significant presence until he died in 1987. A versatile musician, he performed dance music in both continental and North American styles. On his CKUA radio program, *Continental Musicale*, he presented a variety of dance recordings, primarily from European traditions (Figs. 205, 206).

Figure 204 – Haas and his Barndance gang, 1951.

Courtesy O. Sveen

Figure 205 – Haas jams with Olaf Sveen, late 70s or early 80s. The two master accordianists recorded and performed together.

NA 856-2

Figure 206

Ma Trainor led ensembles in Calgary from 1912 until the mid-forties. Like many other Calgary musicians, she frequently played for dances in outlying areas and is widely remembered in the local histories. A sophisticated musician, she was able to front orchestras of several different types. Trainor was a beloved figure to many young Albertans, as late as the Second World War (Figs. 206, 207).

NA 856-4

Figure 207 — ca. 1941.

PB 769–1

Figure 208 – The earliest Old Timer ensemble.
Si Hopkins plays the accordian at the left. Seated in front of him is Roy Watts on guitar; Watt's large hands
were particularly useful to him when he stepped up to the piano. The banjoist at the right is Ernie Yardley.
The accordianist behind Yardley is Lawrence Eidland, a prominent Calgary musician for some years.
This charming hand-tinted photograph was displayed in Tony Neidermayer's study until his death in the late
80s, when it went to the Glenbow Museum.

Calgary orchestras [including the Ma Trainor and Si Hopkins outfits] were hired as buildings became larger and crowds more dense. This was necessitated by the desire for sufficient volume of sound which could only be supplied by a greater number of musicians, or wind instruments. In any case, the age of jazz had arrived, and home-based musicians more or less welcomed the opportunity to regain dancing time lost to them in by-gone years. Some of them still play quite often, and to a full hall. **Trails to the Bow**.

I danced to Ma Trainor's music when I was 16, and when I was at the dance I used to watch the banjo player, and I said to Ma, 'I wish I could play the banjo like that.' Over 25 years later, I was playing for her at a dance in the Crowsnest Pass, and she turned on the piano stool and said, 'You're the best banjo player I ever played with.' Sure made me feel good. Ernie Yardley, "My Life Was Not Wasted In Useless Things."

Depending on how you choose to count, the **CFCN Old Timers** may have been on the air longer than any other program in the history of radio, except for the Metropolitan Opera broadcast from New York. The Old Timers were really more than one group, although there was overlap among the different incarnations. The earliest versions were led by Si Hopkins, accordionist and mandolin-banjo

NA 1616–11

Figure 209 – One 1930s Old Timers lineup. Left to right: Elmer Peck (bass), Eric Watts (violin), Doug Crowdale (guitar and cowboy songs), Si Hopkins (leader, accordion), Bill Tritter (piano), Ernie Yardley (banjo and popular songs), Roy Watts (guitar), Doug Moody (violin).

player. Hopkins's name was in fact Fred Hopkinson — the nickname was initially a joke by guitarist/ pianist/ reedman Roy Watts, standing at the right in the photo above. Watts and Hopkinson had been listening to the Grand Ol' Opry and affecting hill-billy accents; Fred became *Si* and Roy became *Pappy*; both nicknames stuck.

Si Hopkins eventually broke away from the station, and Pappy Watts took over the orchestra. According to one story, Pappy's taste for jazz did not endear him to the station owners or to the bulk of the audience for an old time music program, and the self-confident young accordion virtuoso Tony Neidermayer was given the leadership of the group and the show. (Look for Tony on page 101 as a youngster with a less flashy accordion [Fig. 218] sitting on a motorcycle in Lethbridge.)

> *Waltzes, anything of the day. Ragtime, two-steps. No jazz. Jazz was out.... We played a little bit. If somebody asked for it, we played the 'The Twelfth Street Rag.' We played it once, but we wouldn't play it again. Tony Neidermayer, interviewed by G. W. Lyon, "The CFCN Old Timers: Part Two."*

Figure 210 – Here's Neidermayer in Calgary in 1936...

NA 5411–1

NA 5411-2

Figure 211 — ...and five years later, in the studio as Old Timer leader.

Figure 212 — The CFCN Old Timers in 1953.
Left to right: Tony Neidermayer (leader, accordion), Lint Sadler (bass), Max Morgan and Don Thomas (announcers), Ernie Yardley (banjo), George Fitzsimmons (violin), Nan Tingle (piano). The group proudly wears satin shirts made for them as part of a promotion by a local Singer sewing machine dealer. The Old Timers program did not go off the air until 1981.

Musical Instruments in Portraiture

Since the invention of portraiture, people have chosen to be painted and photographed with prized objects, which they felt somehow defined them. These objects are frequently musical instruments.

Courtesy J. Adams

Times to Remember

Figure 215 – Joe Stein of Acadia Valley with a very beautiful guitar, an instrument which would command a good price among collectors now. Stein died in the 1918 flu epidemic.

NA 4093-27

Figure 214 – Joe Adams in Peace River in the late forties. A guitar with this decorated metal pan on the soundboard is called *resophonic*. Under the pan, one usually finds some sort of metal cone (or set of cones) to amplify the sound; the resophonic guitar was invented before the electric guitar. The unique sound of this instrument (often called the Dobro after one early manufacturer) has come back into favor in many forms of music. Unfortunately, the pan on this particular guitar was a sham. Adams ordered the guitar from a mail order catalog; when it arrived, he discovered that it was a normal wooden guitar with a decorative metal pan screwed onto it. Perhaps this accounts for Joe's serious expression in this photo.

Across the Smoky

Figure 213 – Rocky Mountain House, ca. 1913. The walls are stamped sheet metal, and the bed doesn't look particularly inviting, but the mandolin and carefully trimmed beard give this man, whose name seems long lost, an element of dignity and refinement.

Figure 216 – A dashing young Tom Hubert, showing off his button accordion, pencil mustache & brilliantined hair while sitting atop a boxcar. Hoboes were sometimes known as the Knights of the Road, and while not everyone appreciated their image, they were often seen as romantic, footloose characters.

Figure 217 – Ben Street with an older style of accordion, homesteading in the Cardston area eleven years earlier. The two-row accordion may have been as fully chromatic as Neidermayer's piano model, but it would have been trickier to operate, and had fewer bass notes and chords, which are operated by the spoons on his left hand side. Nevertheless, this was probably a fairly expensive instrument.

Figure 218 – Tony Neidermayer, who led the CFCN Old Timers from 1940 to 1981, as a young man in Lethbridge, with two symbols of modern times in 1927: a piano accordion with 12 basses and a new Harley Davidson motorcycle. He owned the accordion but borrowed the cycle for the photo.

Figure 219 – Of course, a group of utter nonplayers might simply grab their friends' instruments for a gag picture, a common occurrence after the camera became widespread. These Hudson's Bay Co. employees were fooling around in 1928.

Figure 220 – Music making, like any activity, is subject to parody – and while the fiddler and accordionist in this photograph are probably genuine players, and we've encountered a tub used as a drum on page 72, one has doubts about the broom-guitar, the saucepan-banjo, or the mock-bagpiper at the lower right. These are members of the Parkkari family of Alderson, in 1912. The Parkkaris made music together (see also page 77) and were active, as well as humorous, photographers.

101

Alberta could not avoid the cultural influence...

lberta could not avoid the cultural influence of twentieth-century technology.

Your mention of the gramophone reminded me of many happy hours I spent listening to it. Only the other night, while sitting on the wagon with rations, going up to the Company, I was singing to myself some of the old songs I heard so often at your house. 'How Can I Leave Thee,' 'Star of the East,' &c., came into my mind, and I thought of those times (it seems years ago) when I heard them on the gramophone. So you see I do think of you and the friends I left behind in Ridgewood. By the way, does Charlie ever play the violin now? The other week I had the pleasure of listening to the band of the Coldstream Guards, one of the finest military bands in the world. We were in rest billets at the time, and it was a treat I'll not soon forget.

If I ever hear that record 'Till the Boys Come Home,' on your gramophone, it will bring back many memories of this war. I have heard it played on mouth organs in old, leaky barns crowded with men fresh from the muddy trenches; I have heard it whistled, sung or played in 'dugouts' when we have snatched an hour's respite from duty. I still have the pleasure of looking forward to the time when I shall hear it, while sitting comfortably in your house and looking back to those times as a nightmare that is past. J.S. Eagle (written shortly before his death in WWI), **Ridgewood Community**.

Figure 221 – Crowsnest area, ca. 1920.

Figure 222 — The first Christmas for Scandinavian immigrants to Beaverlodge in 1929.
One has received a gramophone as a present.

Figure 223 — Early radios, which played through earphones, rather than speakers, could be cumbersome. They were, nevertheless, much appreciated; Keith Sanitarium, ca. 1928.

In 1928, I was privileged to hear a gramophone recording of 'Red Wing,' played on violin.... I do not know who the musician was; I heard it in the kitchen of a Saskatchewan farm on a very cold winter's day. The young housewife played this one and only record she had over and over again, in between spooning food into a high-chaired youngster, while my father and the farmer dickered over the purchase of a black angus cow that produced very little milk and kicked like hell when anyone tried to milk her. Martin Rossander, "The Dressings We Put On Our Lives."

Figure 224 — CFCN announcer's equipment, 1939.

Figure 225 – 1940s. Note that Canadian radio did include programing from the U.S.

Figure 226 – CFCN broadcasting studio, 1940s.

Although a few Albertans, notably Wilf Carter, had been able to get recording contracts in Montreal or New York, it was not until the second half of the century that Albertans were able to use recordings to transmit their music to each other. Carter's 78s were prized and widely circulated, as were the LPs of Tony Neidermayer's Old Timers some years later, but there were few other regional performers who were able to record. Prior to 1950, the phonograph, like sheet music before it, brought the culture of the outside world to the province, setting standards and

presenting ideas from elsewhere (and possibly enforcing a degree of national and even continental conformity). CDs and tapes still function this way, of course, though now they also carry the messages of many Alberta musicians around the province and to the rest of the world.

On the other hand, in those days radio provided *more* local expression than it does at present. Proof that Albertans used the radio to talk to each other is the role of William Aberhart's broadcasts in the

A1812

Figure 227 – University of Alberta radio studio, 1926.

success of the Social Credit party. Prior to the end of the Second World War, radio most commonly broadcast live, including music which was generally the work of local performers, even though these locals might have been imitating music from elsewhere.

W.W. Grant, who created the original CKUA broadcast facilities, was able to boost the signal of commercial station CFCN so that, on a good day, it was heard as far away as New Zealand; the station received the response cards to prove it. Thanks to the station's powerful signal, which it bragged about on billboards, rural families throughout the northern plains were able, for several decades, to roll up their rugs on Friday or Saturday night to dance to the music of the Old Timers for over 40 years.

Of course, Grant wasn't the only radio genius at work in North America. WLS in Chicago, for example, was nicknamed, "World's Largest Station," and one heard yarns in the southern States that its signal was so strong that it could be picked up from barbed-wire fences! Albertans were able to catch broadcasts from far away, and they were influenced by what they heard. Roy Watts, for instance, spoke of hearing a 1940s broadcast from a U.S. jailhouse, or so he remembered, of a jazzy guitar performance of "Red Wing" and "Listen to the Mockingbird," which caused him to hear these tunes in a new way. His own work was affected by such experiences.

Figure 228 – CKUA record library, 1951.

*On winter nights we had lots of fun dancing at our place and at the Grass home with music supplied by CFCN radio in Calgary. There were never enough women for partners, so we put aprons on some of the men so every one could get a chance to dance. Annie Mills, **Munson and District**.*

Radio station CKUA has long helped to shape Alberta's culture. Created as part of the University of Alberta extension program in 1927, CKUA manifested until recently Alberta's longstanding public commitment to education and cultural development. Many Albertans owe the station a great debt for introducing them to a genre they later came to understand and love, whether it was classical European music, jazz, blues, or exotic musics from around the world. The music Albertans *make* has always been influenced by the music Albertans *have heard*.

Making Music at Home (and Work)

Making music at home...

Figure 229 – Bob & Don Ross, Elnora.

Figure 230 – Two mounties show how they spend their leisure hours in productive artistic pursuit.

Figure 231 – Erickson, Gronet, Hedlund Orchestra, an early ensemble from the Galahad area. The autoharp, played here by the woman at the centre of the photo, is a mechanized zither, which can be played with a minimum of training to provide a chordal accompaniment to a vocalist or instrumental lead. It was invented in the late nineteenth century and sold via an extensive network of travellers who would include brief music lessons in the purchase price. The autoharp was a blessing to someone, in this case probably the wife, who didn't want to be left out of the musical fun, and to aspiring schoolteachers who had no musical background but were called upon to include music in the curriculum. Most players are satisfied to strum chords, but, in a few regions in the southeastern U.S., complicated self-accompanied melodic styles were developed by the 1930s. During the seventies, these techniques were carried throughout the continent.

A6675

Figure 232 – The Bilodeau Family, Beaumont, 1927, show off concertina, fiddle, and either harmonica or comb-and-tissue paper. The latter, sometimes found in a commercial form as the metal or plastic kazoo, can also be given the more dignified musico-logical term, *mirliton*.

NA 2061-2

Figure 234 – The Skjevelin brothers, Cereal, 1915. Scandinavian musicians love the multikeyed, many-rowed, button accordion, which they call the *dragspel*. Here's an early version of the instrument which Olaf Sveen later made famous throughout western Canada. (See Sveen on pages 81 and 95). The instrumentation of this Scandinavian-Albertan trio is startlingly reminiscent of the common ensemble of the Louisiana Cajuns. The cast iron triangle, however, is a common percussion instrument found as far away as India and dating back in Europe at least to the Middle Ages.

NA 4198-3

Figure 233 – Homegrown music is sometimes performed on more or less matched instruments, such as these two plectrum banjos, probably in Turner Valley during the 1920s.

The most common situation for music at home may well have been the singsong at the piano, an event which was rarely photographed (but see Fig. 269, page 130). Al Colton, however, drew a cartoon version for the pages of **The Pathfinders**. A trained (and commercially successful) artist, Colton included a visual quote from the American painter Thomas Hart Benton in the form of the guitarist to the group's right.

*We had a small organ with us on which Margaret, age eleven, could play hymns as well as other music [ca. 1908]. On one evening, which I remember vividly, thirteen cowboys came to our home. They sat on the tables and floor, or wherever they could find a space in our two room shack. They were the Circle Ranch Riders, who were hungry for music and singing. What a night of singing it was, as some of them were real good singers. Others played mouth organs or harmonicas. We didn't have much in the way of cakes or cookies, but mother made a lunch of her wonderful homemade bread, butter, jam and coffee. From then on two or three of the cowboys used to stop in often for a bit of singing or a visit. Frank Durston and Margaret Campbell, **Snake Valley**.*

The Pathfinders

Figure 235 — John Jamieson of Calgary with his wife Evelyn, 1988. John's mother purchased this German instrument in Inverness, in the Scottish Highlands, and sent it to John's brother Alex, who was then living on a farm near Lethbridge. Alex was a dance musician, but John played mostly the Scottish tunes of his father, such as "The Gay Gordons," "I Belong to Glasgow," and "Ca' The Yowes to the Nowes."

Making music at work...

Courtesy M. Rossander

Figure 236 — A collection of amateur musicians, all single men at work on the Lake Louise-Jasper highway in 1935. The dapper fellow with the violin was Danish; he played the classics. The skinny youngster at the far left with the button accordion was also a Dane, but he could not read a note of music. This is Martin Rossander, whose exclamation of delight gave this book its subtitle. None of these men could, or at any rate did, play with each other. The gentleman with the phonograph bought all of Wilf Carter's 78s as they were issued; he and Carter were both popular with these teamsters.

Figure 237 — Often the most joyful occasions were quite informal, perhaps a singsong at a piano when someone had dropped by or a quick jam session after the chores were done, such as this one on the Hallett farm near Edgerton.

Winds of Change

A7641

Figure 238 — At the sawmill, Amber Portage, 1929.

D.C.

NB 16-336

Figure 239 – An impromptu stepdance to an *air fiddler* and hand clapping during lunch break on a buffalo roundup at Wainwright during the late twenties.

Country music has a presence in Alberta...

midst this wealth of influences upon music in the province, it seems ironic to hear (as one does from time to time) country music discussed as somehow "essentially" Albertan. This is no more reasonable than to suggest that the Weadickville shootemups at the Calgary Stampede represent a common experience of the average citizen of the province, in old times or new. Country music has a presence in Alberta, just as it does across Canada, though it would be a mistake to assume that because the Alberta economy includes farming and ranching, Albertans have a greater affinity with the genre than do Newfoundlanders, Quebecers, Ontarians, or British Columbians, all of whom produce their own styles of country music.

This imagined relationship of country music and Alberta is based in large degree on the image of the cowboy, which is shared by both the musical idiom and the province. Country music was originally described as the expression of "hillbillies," but by the fifties, that association was generally avoided because it seemed derogatory. Indeed, cowboy imagery has become very significant to farmers and other rural workers, who've adopted cowboy boots, jeans, and western shirts as their preferred clothing for work and pleasure. I once had a wizened old fellow in Tees, dressed head to toe in a black outfit that reminded me of the movie cowboy, Lash Larue, look me dead in the eye and declare, "I'm a *farmer*!"

Figure 240 – Though the role of "hillbilly" lacks dignity, it did not disappear from the Alberta scene, as can be seen in this photograph of Stampede midway entertainers, from 1944.

Of course, like all other sorts of Albertans, cowboys make music...

Figure 241 – Jarboe Ranch, Red Deer River country, ca. 1912.

NA 2107-2

Figure 242 – Red Deer Lake, date uncertain.

...but probably not very often on horseback, though they learned from Gene Autry publicity stills that this made a dandy portrait (Fig. 243).

But what is a cowboy, anyway? Wilf Carter's career demonstrates how difficult terminology can be. Though he and his music have been taken to heart by rural Albertans, especially in the ranching areas, Carter was born in Nova Scotia and lived large portions of his life in Florida and other American states. He was a professional entertainer since the early thirties, and many old timers cherish humorous recollections that indicate that he was

NA 2771-1

Figure 243 – Wilf Carter, ca. 1932.

perhaps not entirely competent as an agricultural worker. But he did come to Alberta as a young man, he did work on several ranches and did compete in the Stampede (performing the unappetizing chore of "earing down" — biting the ear to keep the horse still so it could be saddled for the wild bronc race), and he maintained his Alberta connection, spending most summers here and keeping stock. He's probably about as close to a real cowboy as you'll find in country music.

Pete Knight [the rodeo bronc rider] and I was great buddies. He took me out of [the
rodeo] by shakin' hands behind the chutes one day and promisin' that I would not do it any more. 'Cause I used to play the guitar and all kinds of stuff for the cowboys, Pete Knight and Herman Linder and all the great boys. So I shook hands with him, and I quit. Wilf Carter, interviewed by G.W. Lyon, "We Shook Hands."

On the way home, I stopped at Webb's music shop on 17th Avenue and bought a $6.00 ukelele. I taught myself to strum it and learned the chords. That started me in the musical do at the Hitching Post theatre with

Figure 244 – Carter at the 1989 Calgary Folk Festival, his last performance in Calgary. He shares a musical moment with bassist Cindy Church, who has herself made a strong impact as a Canadian country singer.

Wilf Carter and a black man by the name, I believe, of Arnold Biggs. Myself singing with the uke, Biggs stepdancing, and Wilf yodelling. I went the first time on a dare, and a bet of five bucks. That was the real start of the music. When I think back, it seems almost unbelievable that I had the nerve to go ahead and teach myself to read, write and play.

...I played an S.S. Stewart guitar when I sang popular songs opposite Wilf Carter. He sang cowboy songs and I sang pops for 13 years on the radio and in the halls; we played all over Alberta and into B.C. Ernie Yardley, "My Life Was Not Wasted In Useless Things."

In Alberta, everybody seems to want to be a cowboy ... especially during Stampede Week in Calgary.

Figure 245 – Cast of a Bnai B'rith revue, Calgary, 1951.

Figure 246 – Calgary Safety Roundup Singers, ca. 1972.

Figure 247– Verna Narolsky, who broadcast over CJCA in Edmonton and CJCJ and CFCN in Calgary, Edmonton, ca. 1936.

NA 4727–4

P3929

Figure 248 – CFCN "cowgirl" singers from the Burns Chuckwagon Radio Program, Calgary, 1940. I'll bet *they* never eared down a wild bronc, at least not anywhere near the ol' corral!

Figure 249 — The Hungarian Gypsy Orchestra at the Tokay Restaurant, on a regular night in the 1950s...

Figure 250 — ...and during Stampede.

Compare the elaborate Hungarian dulcimer to portable Ukrainian variety seen in many photographs.

Some Albertans like to play at Indians instead of cowboys, which sometimes annoys the Native people themselves and often looks ridiculous (Fig. 252).

The term *country and western* was invented after World War Two to stress the commonalities between the music heard on such radio stations as Tennessee's WSM (the home of the Grand Ol' Opry) and the *western swing* of Texas and California. To this mix, other elements — honky tonk, rockabilly, and various "ethnic" musics — have frequently been added. The association of country music and cowboys waxes and wanes, but never disappears.

But there have been countless country and "cowboy" musicians in Alberta since World War II — and *they're all good!*

Figure 251 — Thomas Wilson, a farmer near Leavitt at the turn of the century.

Figure 252 — An important early figure in Alberta country music was tenor banjoist Ray Little, who came to Calgary from New Hampshire during the thirties to work in radio. His listenable music, now only available on long deleted lps to be found only in garage sales and flea markets, deserves to be revived.

Figure 253 — Stampede Week, 1962. Steel guitar player Chuck Kuntz and electric bass player Johnny Chabros worked extensively with Roy Warhurst, and Cliff Kadatz, television's "Tumbleweed."

Figure 254 — Calgary Stampede, July 1988.

NA 5093–996

Figure 255 – J.B. Ham and the Sons of the South were featured on CFCN during the 1940s.

NA 2771-14

Figure 256 – Unknown musicians, probably in Edmonton, 1958.

PA2481/1

Music is Essential at Weddings (and Elsewhere)

Music is essential at weddings...

Weddings were usually held during the winter, when the farmers had more free time. "After the ceremony, the party returned to the home of the bride, where they were greeted by volley after volley of shotguns.

"After the wedding supper was served, the room was cleared for dancing. Among the dances performed at such an occasion were the Square Dance, Reel of Eight, Reel of Four,

Drops of Brandy, French Minuet, the Waltz, Duck Dance, Jig, Quadrille, Schottische, and the Circassian Circle. The music for the dance was supplied by the local violinists accompanied by someone on organ. When a jig was played, there was always keen competition between the men and the women to see who could perform the greatest variety of jig steps. Contrasting sharply with the soft rhythmic

Figure 257 – Pincher Creek, undated.

NA 2539-4

Figure 258 — Crowsnest area, 1920s.

Figure 259 — A wedding procession from Crowsnest Pass, 1920s. Once upon a time, the wedding march began as the procession to the church and ended with a parade to the reception. Anyone who has lived near a city park during June would wish for a return to a musical accompaniment, rather than the bleating of car horns! Note the cello strapped to the player's shoulder, so he can play as he strolls.

124

shuffle of those in the jig who wore moccasins was the louder scrape of the dancers who wore hard leather shoes. The dust that was being raised, meantime, by the energetic dancers, often became so thick it was necessary to call a halt once or twice during the evening to sweep the floor. After continuing till early morning, the wedding celebration would draw to a close and horses were once again hitched to sleighs that would take the guests home to their rest." Frank E. Mitchell, **A History of Pioneering in the Pakan District**.

The Doctor's Dance (Local newspaper — September 1920).

"At Doc Roger's dance last night there was a large crowd. This was expected, as the dance was free; not to mention the glad occasion it commemorated — the doctor's wedding. That this fact was remembered was evident in every phase and feature of the affair: — The lights burned brighter, the floor had an extra shake of powder on its face; so did the girls; the cornet and trombone artists had their horns polished. Sally had a new ribbon in her hair, and Hillier at the piano kept his foot on the gas pedal and let her rip. Everybody danced who could and some who couldn't. We don't want to mention names; we might get hit; but there were as many varieties of dancing as there were styles of hair. Some kept up a perpetual wobble as if they were itchy. Some twisted about like snakes in pain; some took the matter calmly and appeared to be walking

in their sleep while others cantered all over the hall. The bride had the unfortunate function to perform of dancing with every man, and did her part like a heroine. How she learned so many ways of doing the same dance baffles us. The doctor had the happier lot of dancing with every girl, but as he had danced with them all before that was nothing new." **Yesterday and Years Ago**.

Ukrainian country weddings carried a reputation in a class by themselves for conviviality, good food and merriment to which Dad contributed several years of his skill on the violin. He was usually accompanied by others skilled on an accordion and dulcimer. William E. 'Buck' Buchanan of the Alberta Provincial Police Detachment in Smoky Lake, often participated with his drums when occasion would release him from his duties, rapping out a staccato up-beat tempo that was certain to stimulate a crashing foot stamp to the floor by the males, whilst the ladies' 'soft shoe' dipped into the beat as only the grace of a female dancer allows it. All this was rendered in the way that a 'Hopak' was intended, as a sure fire cure-all for rheumatic or work weary muscular aches. In the stimulating atmosphere of these events the 'E' string on Dad's violin frequently broke as he enthusiastically laid his bow to the tune. He always carried a couple of spares in his pocket. William Chahley, **Our Legacy**.

for funerals...

NA 4279-7

Figure 260 – Crowsnest Pass, 1920s.

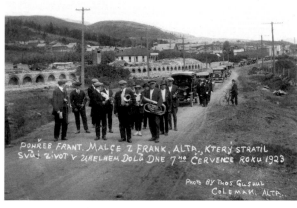

NC 54-2814

Figure 261 – Frank, 1925.

other ceremonies...

Choir practice kept me busy and many a cold night I walked from and back to West Carbon. The hardest thing we ever were called on to do was sing in a trio at Annie Douglas' *funeral in 1941. Hard to keep back the tears as the hymn chosen was 'Breathe on Me, Breath of God.'* **Carbon: Our History Our Heritage**.

NA 3368-18

Figure 262 – Bringing the Torah into the synagogue, Calgary, 1940s.

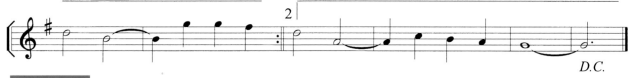

D.C.

Figure 263 — Fête des Rois (Epiphany) at Red Deer, January 6, 1915.

Figure 264 — Mandolin orchestra playing for a Communist gathering in Crowsnest Pass, ca. 1920. The banner over their heads offers an exhortation to the Proletariat.

...and at picnics and events whose occasion has long been forgotten.

Figure 265 — Crowsnest area, 1915.

Figure 266 — Crowsnest area, ca. 1920.

Figure 267 – A picnic at Acadia Valley, probably during the thirties.

Figure 268 – A party of Royalite Co. employees, Turner Valley, ca. 1950.

129

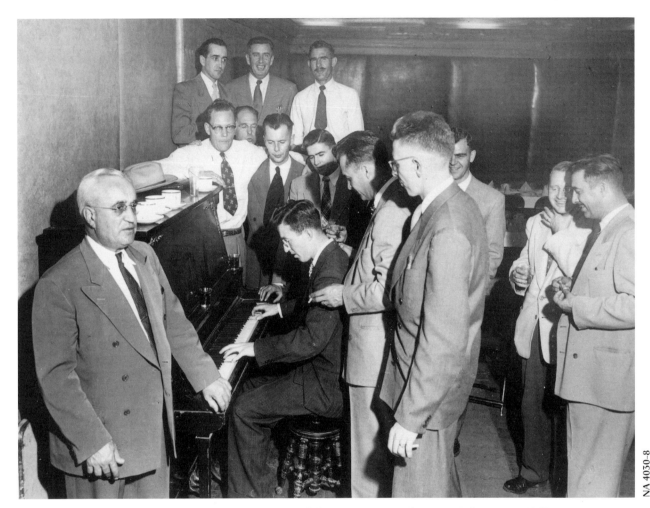

Figure 269 – Alberta pharmacists and drug company salesmen, Calgary, ca. 1942.

NA 4030-8

Native people participate in mainstream culture...

Like many other Canadian groups, Native people not only participate in mainstream culture, but also have their own, which they have retained and developed despite a variety of pressures (often including government policy) that they assimilate to European Canadian society.

The joy of rediscovering our traditional identity is visible to all. Our colors are brighter, our movements are sharper, our competitive spirit is stronger than ever before. In the Inter-Tribal Dance, we call on all the tribes of North America to share our happiness. **Calgary '88 Pow Wow**.

Aboriginally, the role of music in Native communities was rather different than among Europeans. For one thing, Natives had less interest in developing a large variety of instruments. As in many other cultures (notably south Asia, Siberia, and parts of Africa), the drum was recognized as a spiritually potent instrument, not merely as a timekeeper. Voice and drum (often working together in complex polyrhythms) were found quite sufficient to create moving, uplifting, and spiritually effective music; this preference has been supplemented by new musical interests, but it is still important in Native culture.

Adam finishes talking and offers to sing. His voice merges with the sound of his drum, rising and falling with the cadence that makes Dene singing so distinctive. His last, high note hangs in the air like the smell of smoke from a campfire. Silence fills the room and no one —

not I, nor Maggie, my interpreter —feels like talking as we hold the sounds of the song in our minds. Though Adam sings in a language different from mine, it is obvious the song's words are deeply significant to him.

Finally, he breaks the silence and explains he felt deep emotion while singing. He confirms the song is special; it is the one his father sang for his mother before she died. Dianne Meili, "Adam Salopree: Dene Tha', Meander River Reserve," **Those Who Know**.

Native music was traditionally defined in more functional terms than is common in European-derived music. Europeans recognize musical items by form: the differences between sonatas and suites, waltzes and quadrilles, and ballads and blues are matters of structure first, and then, perhaps to a lesser degree, of mood. Among many Native groups, however, songs were defined by purpose: lullabies are different from war songs, the song for a chicken dance is different from that for a tobacco ritual, not so much because of the form or musical content of each, but because of their social or personal uses.

Much Native music is associated with specific ritual functions, which may include processions (Figs. 270, 277, 279), sweat lodges (Figs. 272, 274), and the hand game (Figs. 275– 276) – exciting and puzzling to outsiders, but of spiritual significance among many Native nations.

There's a spiritual meaning behind everything at the Tea Dance,' explains Molly. 'The

Figure 270 – Medicine Pipe Transfer, Blackfoot Sun Dance, 1920s.

NA 667-231

Figure 271 – Tsuu T'ina Beaver Bundle Ceremony, 1920s.

NA 667-774

NA 667-640

Figure 272

NA 1481-106

Figure 275 – Hand game at the Siksika Sun Dance, 1961.

NA 4897-10

Figure 276 – Blood players at the Tsuu T'ina Indian Days, mid-sixties.

NA 667-642

Figure 273)

NA 667

Figure 274 – Tsuu T'ina sweat lodge, probably 1920s.

NA 1481-533

Figure 277 – Members of the Horn Society dance in front of Holy Woman's sun shade, Blackfoot Sun Dance, 1961.

NA 991–29

Figure 278 — All Smoke Ceremony at the home of Ben Calf Robe, Blackfoot Reserve, 1959.

NA 667-254

Figure 279 — Horn Society, Blackfoot Sundance, ca. 1927.

drum represents the circle of life. It's made of an animal skin and wood, the Creator's gifts to us, and you have to heat it up near fire for it to sound good. There's a real power behind it. The drum brings people together and awakens something. When you hear it and dance, it's a way of expressing yourself,

rejoicing. You realize you have this powerful connection between yourself, the Creator, and everyone else. If you're at a Tea Dance, you just don't want to sit down. Dianne Meili, "Alexis Seniantha: Dene Tha', Assumption Reserve," **Those Who Know**.

NA 667-222

Figure 280 — Prairie Chicken Society dance, at the Blackfoot Sun Dance, probably 1940s.

NA 667-1053

Figure 281 — Grass Dance, at the Blood Sun Dance, ca. 1940s.

Of course, one important function of the dance, as of any cultural activity, is sheer delight (Figs. 280, 281)!

Grass Dance: We honor Mother Earth by adorning our clothes with grass and swaying in the prairie wind. **Calgary '88 Pow Wow.**

The Prairie Chicken Dance: It is the duty of the Prairie Chicken Society to see that all members of the tribe have enough for their survival. Once, some of our hunters stopped in their travels to admire the prairie chicken's mating dance. As they watched, warriors from another tribe attacked and killed the hunters. The prairie chickens told our People who had done the killing so that the young men could be avenged. The Prairie Chicken Society honored the prairie chicken by taking its name and following its movement in their dance. **Calgary '88 Pow Wow.**

Figure 282 — Young women at St. Mary's School kept up with the trends. Blood Reserve, 1940s.

Figure 283 — Anna Beaver and the Stony Indian All Girls Brass Band at the Calgary Stampede, 1944.

Native people have always been receptive to the new instruments and musical ideas that Europeans brought them, though often, as in the residence schools, the circumstances of the encounter were traumatic. The religious educators who introduced Native students to the mandolin, the violin, and the piano hoped that the love of these instruments and the ensemble experience would lead their charges to the classical music of Europe, which so often speaks of Christian devotion. Presumably this sometimes occurred. But as often as not, this musical education, among other acculturating experiences, presented young Natives with an entrance into popular music, especially country and rock, and into their personal creativity as North Americans.

> *About 1915, a theatre was built. It was in business for a while and closed. The building was then used as a dance hall where big 'moochigans' (Cree for dance) were held. A two piece orchestra consisting of a fiddle and someone chording on the piano furnished the music. The Indian elders sat on benches along the walls and did a shuffle in time to the music. Siddon Key,* **Pioneers Who Blazed the Trail***.*

In particular, the Métis encounter with the European fiddle has produced music that is so distinctive that some observers feel that this style characterizes western Canadian fiddling, perhaps with some significant influence from Ukrainian techniques. The Manitoban Métis Andy deJarlis is sometimes said to occupy the role in western fiddling that Don Messer has in other regions of the country.

It's important to realize that when Native people took up European musical instruments and forms, they adapted them to their own purposes. The older styles of fiddle music among Natives and Métis, in particular, are specific to those cultures, not merely poor imitations of European originals. Anne Lederman, who has studied this music in Manitoba, noted, "The French-Canadian roots of the music are obvious, especially in the vigourous bowing and the tapping of both feet to emphasize the rhythm. However, the uneven lengths of the phrases and the way the tunes are constructed owe much to the Native heritage of the musicians and make this style of fiddling unique in North America."

In many cases, tunes are "reconstructed," since Native fiddlers are playing their own versions of tunes that already exist. Lederman notes, "To many people, Native and non-Native alike, the old tunes are considered to have 'crazy rhythm.'" That is, not everyone is comfortable with the way melodies were reshaped to this new sensibility. This is probably the context in which we should read the following comment from an Alberta local history.

> *One of the favorite tunes on the fiddle was 'Red Wing.' We used to laugh at Louis Houle. He used to cut the corners. He left Red Wing out in the cold several times.* **Ten Dollars and a Dream***.*

Lederman acknowledges that many younger Native and Métis fiddlers are moving away from

A8125

Figure 284 – ca. 1900

NC 6-12750(e)

Figure 285 – Métis dance troupe at a fair held at Edmonton, 1930. Their costumes seem to include wigs; in their daily lives, they probably kept their hair short, as did everyone else on the streets.

NA 5127-5

Figure 286 – Grand Centre, 1940s.

Figure 287 – Lac La Biche Pow Wow Days, July 1965.

PA363/15

NA 5127-6

Figure 288 – Grand Centre, probably 1950s.

these older styles, but there are also a handful of young European Canadian fiddlers (Calvin Vollrath in Alberta and Patti Kusturok in Manitoba in particular) who've learned to play in Métis fashion, as, indeed, has Lederman herself. Lederman's two elegantly produced recordings of Native and Métis fiddling from Manitoba have also served to give to this tradition some of the respect it deserves.

After lunch [at the dance] the singing would begin. 'Hopey,' a Canadian from way back, sang Newfoundland ballads in a mournful voice. Henry Scheper and the Siemer brothers would sing well-loved German melodies, their voices brimming with emotion. The Métis boys were much applauded: 'Sing! Sing!' They would strum on guitars and banjos and with dark eyes flashing, sing and yodel cowboy songs popular at the time: 'Strawberry Roan,'

139

A2142

Figure 289 – This photo from the Provincial Archives is captioned, "Indian party near Whyte Avenue, Edmonton," which seems misleading, since they were almost certainly invited to perform for some urban event. The photograph is not dated but is obviously rather old.

'Lonesome Cowboy,' 'When the Work's All Done This Fall,' and the tear-jerking 'My Father was a Drunkard.'

These sons of the Métis settlers who lived in the district, and whose small brothers and sisters were our classmates, seemed to us romantic characters. Everyone knew that the dances could not have taken place without them, as they provided the music, the square dance caller and a lot of the action on the dance floor. Mary B. Mark, **Dreams Become Realities**.

There are few dances in the world which combine vigor and grace as delightfully as does the Red River Jig, a dance and tune that clearly reveal their complex intercultural heritage (Fig. 287).

Since the earliest days, Native people have been happy to share many aspects of their culture with the newcomers. This came naturally to them, since borrowing among nations was always an important factor for change in Native cultures.

But no dance was complete without the Red River Jig, that had to be done in moccasins as it was by the Métis of the Red River Valley. In the 1880's, this dance was after midnight entertainment; from their hip pocket the performers would whip out a pair of light moccasins, which sometimes were mistaken for a flask of hooch to pep them up at midnight. The Red River Jig, the Indian and Métis national dance, was a shuffle that embodied the Irish step dance, and the Highland Fling of the Scotch. It was a marathon dance, starting out slowly; gradually the fiddlers increased the tempo until all but one couple broke step. At some of the old time dances featuring the Red

River Jig, the ladies would come prepared to take part in the marathon, decked out in beautiful white doeskin dressed with beadwork design and wearing their favorite flower. John Julius Martin, **The Prairie Hub***.*

At times, we take or transfer the dances of others. We traded or adapted these dances among the different Native people. Indian Nations are once again celebrating their cultures and asserting their pride by dancing and proclaiming their achievements and heritage. **Calgary '88 Pow Wow***.*

Certainly there are limits to what they will share and what can be changed — among all peoples, Natives and others, religious and certain social ceremonies (marriage, for instance) deserve the kind of privacy that preserves the solemnity of the occasion. But whites are welcome to secular Pow Wows, and Native dancers have been fixtures at public events — on the streets and in school gymnasiums — since the province's cities were founded.

Louise Big Plume's parents were at that first Stampede [in 1912]. The 81-year-old Elder with the Tsuu T'ina Nation still gets her family to set up a tipi at the Indian Village. The tipi has the same red and white design as the one her parents set up years ago.

Big Plume has been part of the village pretty much every July since 1932, and says the biggest changes are how expensive everything is, and how much junk food is available!

There are still a lot of misconceptions about Indians, she adds. Big Plume has been asked by tourists from Holland, Australia, and England whether she can speak English or read and write. Carla Turner, "Indian Village offers a glimpse of life in tipis."

The presence of new people on the continent led Native people to redefine themselves. Now, in addition to their own national distinctions, they came to understand themselves as "Indians." The increased communication and travel possibilities of the twentieth century — in which Natives partake with great delight — has led "Indians" to develop an entirely new cultural medium, the Pow Wow.

At a Pow Wow, Natives from many nations, many regions, gather to share music, dance, food (*This car brakes for frybread!*), and other cultural and social activities. Some Pow Wow dancers favor clothing and dance steps particular to their own nations, but there are a variety of Pan-Indian costumes and dancing styles: most prominently Traditional, Fancy, and Grass dance.

Pow Wow dancers dance for the joy of dancing, but also to express and develop old cultural possibilities.

Sometimes we went to the Treaty Days on Saddle Lake Reserve. We would set up a tent for three days alongside our native friends, not wanting to miss a thing that was going on.... In the evening there was Pow Wow dancing, and we were allowed to join in with them to the sounds of drums. Later that evening was dancing to the old time music of Pat Paul and his band from sun-down to sun-up. Helene Cooper and Armand Foisey, **Dreams Become Realities***.*

Grouard was also the base for the Royal North West Mounted Police, then 'the law' for the territory. Corporal Cochran, the officer in charge of the R.N.W.M.P. post, had a young bride who, like me, was a newcomer from the outside. I was invited to be their houseguest and while there, attended some of the post dances. At one dance there was an Indian ceremonial tea dance where both Indians and whites joined hands and danced in a circle doing a kind of one-two shuffle to the beat of Tom-Toms. Della Brown Dixon, **Pioneers Who Blazed the Trail***.*

Figure 290 – Calgary Stampede, 1962. These Native people may be performing at Rope Square or a similar event, or they may be part of the parade, giving a brief performance as the parade stops. Note the European bass drum which has been converted to their own purpose.

Figure 291 – The Chieftains on a float – Lac La Biche Pow Wow Days, July 1965.

Figure 292 – Tsuu T'ina Reserve, Summer 1992.

Figure 293 – Dancers at the Calgary Native Awareness Week Pow Wow, May 1989.

NA 4897-8

Figure 294 — Yellowfly, a Siksika, dancing at the Tsuu T'ina Indian Days during the 1960s.

And like rodeo families, tsymbalists, and old time fiddlers, Native people dance to pay for their vacations. Most Pow Wows include competition dances, the prize money for which can be substantial. Many Pow Wows are held alongside rodeos, either large, inter-ethnic ones like the Stampede, or smaller, Native-oriented ones, such as that held during the Tsuu T'ina Indian Days (Figs. 292, 294).

Note the numbered armbands on some of these dancers, which identify them for the judges. Needless to say, the presence of competition affects the dances themselves, which may be getting more complex — certainly dance clothing is (Fig. 293–296)!

In addition, as ethnomusicologist R. Witmer noted some years ago, Natives are taking advantage of affordable tape recorders to preserve the performances of favorite drum groups (Fig. 297, 298). This will permit them to study performance styles at leisure, a new possibility for this ancient but dynamic music tradition. Who knows what sorts of innovations another century of interaction and evolution will produce?

Courtesy M. Pollock

Figure 295

Courtesy M. Pollock

Figure 296 – Native Awareness Week Competition Pow Wow, Calgary, 1989.

Figure 297 – Drummers and listeners at the Calgary Native Awareness Week Pow Wow, May 1989.

Figure 298

Figure 299 – The Canadian Eagles, 1967. This rock and blues band from Hobbema seems to have had at least a degree of parody in their presentation.

NA 2557-43

PA363/18

Figure 300 – The Chieftains' lineup was similar to that of the surfing bands of the early sixties, such as the Beach Boys and the Astronauts. So was their dress, if you ignore their wigs. Given their age, it's a safe bet that their repertoire included "Surfin' USA," "Little Deuce Coupe," and "Telstar."

While the Native people of Alberta maintain and develop their older expressive forms, they also participate in the cultural venues available to all Canadians.

'Red Wing' was the popular tune of the day, and we played it so often we could almost imagine poor Red Wing down in the cotton wood trees weeping by the side of her camp fire, while her brave warrior beau lay scalped on the field of battle far away. Dr. W. R. Read, **The Hills of Home**.

J1691

Figure 301 — Harry Rusk in 1975. During his long career, Rusk carried the traditional country
music sound from the era of Hank Snow into the 1980s...

J5460/5

Figure 302 — ...and Laura Vinson follows country-rock and related traditions into a new century. The name of her former backup band, Red Wyng, evokes her Métis heritage and the orthographic frenzy of the sixties, as well as the most popular song in Alberta's first hundred years. She has yet to achieve the commercial success of some more fortunate performers, notably kd lang, but she's a dedicated and talented singer. Who knows what the future holds for her? Vinson at the Country Music Festival, Lake Eden, July 4, 1977.

Figure 303 – Rich and the Country Rebel Band. Their repertoire tended to the older styles of the fifties: Hank Williams songs performed to a Johnny Cash beat.

Figure 304 – Two members of Stray Horse, a Treaty Seven band which favored a more contemporary, rockier sound.

If we leave Laura Vinson poised at the possibility of stardom, let's not finish our examination of Alberta's musical history without reminding ourselves that it's not merely the *stars* who are important. Like other groups of Albertans, the Native communities, Treaty and Métis, include many musicians, amateur, part-time, and fully professional, who'll never be famous, but who make honest and often vibrant music and are essential to the cultural lives of their communities and to the province as a whole. Here are two Native country music groups who performed on Stephen Avenue during the 1994 Calgary Stampede (Fig. 303, 304).

Bibliography

General Sources

Calgary '88 Pow Wow: History of Native Peoples Through Native Dance. [Calgary]: Calgary Olympic Association, [1988]. Program.

Carter, Wilf. The Yodelling Cowboy: Montana Slim from Nova Scotia. Toronto; Ryerson, 1961.

Charyk, John C. The Biggest Day of the Year: The Old-Time School Christmas Concert. Saskatoon: Western Producer Prairie Books, 1985.

Cunningham, David. Making Do — A Prairie Memory Guide. Edmonton: Lone Pine Media Productions, Ltd., 1982.

Every Saturday Night. Film. Tom Radford and John Taylor. National Film Board, 1973.

Fowke, Edith. "Anglo-Canadian Folksong: A Survey." Ethnomusicology 16 (1972): 335-349.

Hendrickson, Cheryl J. "English Language Folk Music in Alberta." Canadian Folk Music Journal 10 (1982): 34-39.

Henry, Dave. "Biographical Sketch," Gushul Studio Photographic Collection. Arrangement and Description by Dave Henry. Calgary: Glenbow Archive, n.d.

Jonker, Peter. The Song and the Silence: Sitting Wind, The Life of Stoney Indian Chief Frank Kaquitts. Edmonton: Lone Pine, 1988.

Kelly, L.V. North With Peace River Jim. Introduction and edited by Hugh A. Dempsey. Historical Paper #2. Calgary: Glenbow-Alberta Institute, 1972. (Published originally in Calgary Herald, August 13-October 1, 1910.)

Lederman, Anne. Old Native and Métis Fiddling in Manitoba Volume I. Recording with notes. Toronto: Falcon Productions, 1987.

Lyon, George W. "I'm Olle Myself!: An Interview with Olaf Sveen." Canadian Folk Music Bulletin 28.4 (December 1994): 3-9.

— "The CFCN Old Timers: Part One." Old Time Country 8.4 (Winter 1993): 13-15, 28, 31.

— "The CFCN Old Timers: Part Two." Old Time Country 9.1 and 2 (Spring/Summer 1993): 8-11.

— "Mr. & Mrs. Jamieson, a Waltz." Canadian Folk Music Bulletin 27.2 (June 1993): 39-40.

— "Roy Logan: A Profile." Canadian Folk Music Bulletin 26.4 (Winter 1992). Reprinted in Fiddle News & Views March 1, 1994.

— "Words From The Range: Canadian Cowboy Poetry." Canadian Folk Music Bulletin 25.4 (Winter 1991): 3-12.

— "Fiddling around is serious business." Western People (December 15, 1988): 3.

— "The Prairie Music Box: The Mechanics of Oompah pah." Guitar Canada (Summer 1988): 24-26.

— "We Shook Hands," An Interview with Wilf Carter. Canadian Folk Music Bulletin (June 1987): 5-14. Reprinted in Old Time Country 8.2 (Summer 1992).

— "Some Good Schoolhouse Stuff!' Speculations on Historical Vernacular Culture in Alberta." Foothills Magazine Mount Royal College 3.2 (1987): 5-12.

— Historic Community Music In Alberta, A Survey (1985). Unpublished, available at Alberta Historical Resources Foundation.

Malcom, Peter. "Music in Alberta, Pat One," Alberta Museums Review 8.2 (Fall 1983): 10-12.

Martin, John Julius. The Prairie Hub, An Outline History of Early Western Events. Mrs. Edythe M. Groves, ed. Strathmore, Alberta: Strathmore Standard, 1967.

Meili, Dianne. Those Who Know: Profiles of Alberta's Native Elders. Edmonton: NeWest, 1991.

Nelson, Margaret (Horton). **The Happy Hortons — 1946-1951**. Marwayne, Alberta: Unpublished typescript, 1987.

Paulls, Leonora Mary. **The English Language Folk and Traditional Songs of Alberta: Collection and Analysis for Teaching Purposes**. Master's Thesis, University of Calgary Department of Music, 1981.

Rogers, T.B. "Is There An Alberta Folk Music?" **Canadian Folk Music Journal** 6 (1978): 23-29.

Ross, Toni. **Oh! The Coal Branch**. 2nd Printing. Edmonton: n.p., 1976.

Rossander, Martin."Old-Time Music in Big Hill Country: The Thirties." **Old Time Country** 7.4 (Fall 1991): 14-18.

— "Riding the rails: A boy escapes the Depression." **Western People** (June 9, 1988):10-11.

— "The Dressings We Put On Our Lives." **Canadian Folk Music Bulletin** (September/December 1986): 10-14.

— "A Musician's Memoir." **Fort Calgary Quarterly** 6.4 (1986): 10-11.

— "A Country Dance `back in the hills." **The Cornerstone** 9.1 (1986): 12-13.

Russell, Andy. **Trails of a Wilderness Wanderer**. New York and Toronto: Ballantine, 1970.

Snow, Chief John. **The Stoney Nation Presents Nakoda Olympic Pow-Wow '88**. Morley: Stoney Tribal Administration, 1988.

Spalding, David A.E. "'What We Sang Down on the Farm': A Forgotten Manuscript on Western Canadian Singing Traditions." **Canadian Folk Music Journal** 13 (1985): 37-53.

Turner, Carla. "Indian Village offers a glimpse of life in tipis." **Windspeaker Guide to Indian Country 95** 13.2 June 1995 Guide Page 24

Voisey, Paul. **Vulcan: The Making of a Prairie Community**. Toronto: U of Toronto P, 1988.

Wetherell, Donald G., with Irene Kmet. **Useful Pleasures: The Shaping of Leisure in Alberta 1896-1945**. Regina: Alberta Culture and Multiculturalism/Canadian Plains Research Centre, 1990.

Witmer, Robert. **The Musical Life of the Blood Indians**. Mercury Series, Canadian Ethnology Service Paper 86. Ottawa: National Museum of Man, 1982.

Yardley, Ernie T. "My Life Was Not Wasted In Useless Things." **Canadian Folk Music Bulletin** 23.4 (December 1989): 15-20.

Local Histories

Numbers in parentheses indicate which pages contain contributions from each local history.

Across the Smoky. Fran and Winnie Moore, eds. DeBolt and District Pioneer Museum Society, 1978. (100)

The Battle River Country. J.R.S. Hambly, ed. The Duhamel Historical Society, 1974. (70)

Beaverlodge to the Rockies. E.C. Stacey, ed. Beaverlodge and District Historical Association, 1974. (37)

Beiseker's Golden Heritage. W. and B. Schissel and L. Harty, eds. Beiseker Historical Society, 1977. (69, 78)

Best in the West by a Damsite 1900-1940. Bassano History Book Club, 1974. (91)

Between River and Lake. Pauline Feniak, ed. The Warspite Victoria Trail Historical Society, n.d. (76)

The Big Bend. Wilma K. Bird, ed. Big Bend Historical Committee, 1981. (72)

Building and Working Together: A Study of the Thorhild Area Vol. 1. Thorhild and District Historical Society, 1985. (1)

Buried Treasures: The History of Elnora, Pine Lake and Huxley. Elnora History Committee, 1972. (23)

The Butte Stands Guard. Stavely Historical Book Society, 1976. (58-59)

Candlelight Years. Innisfail and District Historical Society Book Section, 1973. (61)

Carbon: Our History Our Heritage. Muriel Hay, ed. Carbon Historical Committee, 1986. (126)

A Century of Memories: Okotoks and District, **1883-1983**. Okotoks and District Historical Society, 1983. (58)

Cherished Memories. Ardossan Unifarm, 1972. (9)

Donalda's Roots and Branches. U-Go Weaver's History Book Committee, 1980. (22)

Dreams Become Realities: A History of Lafond and Surrounding Areas. The Lafond Historical Committee, 1981. (139-40)

80 Years of Progress. Westlock History Book Committee, 1984. (4)

Fencelines and Furrows. Fencelines and Furrows History Book Society, 1971. (2)

Foley Trail Vol.II. Hazel Fausak, ed. Pembina Lobstick Historical Society, 1984. (29, 62, 89)

From Hoofprints to Highways: Leslieville and Districts Commemorate Alberta's Seventy-Fifth Anniversary Volume Two. Leslieville and District Historical Society, 1980. (69)

Golden Echoes: A History of Galahad and Districts. Galahad Historical Society, 1980. (108)

The Golden Years. Barrhead History Book Committee, 1978. (26)

Grub-Axe To Grain. Spruce View School Area Historical Society Book Committee, 1973. (xi)

Hanna North. Jean James, ed. Hanna North Book Club, 1978. (61-62)

Harvest of Memories. The Majestic-Farnell Lake Women's Committee, 1968. (72)

The Hills of Home. Margaret Playle, ed. Drumheller Valley History Association, 1973. (147)

A History of Pioneering in the Pakan District. Frank E. Mitchell. N.p., n.d. (123-25)

Homestead Country: Wrentham and Area. Wrentham Historical Society, 1980. (57-58)

Homesteads and Happiness. Eckville and District Historical Society, 1979. (63-65)

Land of Red and White. Frog Lake Community Club, 1975. (5, 72, 79)

Lanterns on the Prairie: Strome Diamond Jubilee 1905-1980. Strome Senior Citizens Club, 1980. (59)

Lengthening Shadows of the Neutrals. New Dawn Seniors Club, 1979. (75-76)

M.D. of Kneehill 1904-1967. L. Grace Gore, ed. Municipal District of Kneehill, 1967. (69)

Memories of Fairgrove District. Sedgewick Community Press, 1977. (1-2)

Memories of Mundare: A History of Mundare and Districts. Mundare Historical Society, 1980. (9, 35, 37, 79)

Memories Past to Present: A History of Beaver Crossing and Surrounding District. Cherry Grove History Committee, 1981. (63)

Munson and District. Munson Centennial Book Committee, 1967. (106-07)

Our Huxley Heritage. Eva Jensen, ed. Huxley and District History Book Committee, 1983. (25)

Our Legacy: History of Smoky Lake and Area. Smoky Lake and District Culture and Heritage Society and Town of Smoky Lake, 1983. (59, 125)

The Pathfinders: A History of Onoway, Bilby, Brookdale, Glenford, Goldthorpe, Heatherdon, Hillcrest, Nakamun, Rich Valley. Speldhurst, Stettin, and Sturgeon River. Elizabeth Turnbull and Jean Payne, eds. The Onoway Women's Institute, 1978. (30, 110)

Pioneers Who Blazed the Trail. Centennial Book Committee, F.W.V.A. High Prairie Local 204, 1967. (137, 141)

Red Willow Reflections. The Red Willow Pioneer Book Committee, 1981. (62)

Reflections: A History of Elk Point and District. Mary Bennett, ed. The Elk Point and District Historical Society, 1977. (4-6)

Ridgewood Community Red Deer Alberta 1889-1967. Ruby V. Bickley, ed. The Ridgewood Women's Institute, 1967. (103)

Shortgrass Country: A History of Foremost and Nemiskam. Alyce Butterwick, ed. Foremost Historical Society, 1975. (2, 88)

Sibbald Community History: 1908-1980. Sibbald Community Club, 1980. (59-61)

Silver Sage Bow Island 1900-1920. Jack Thomas, ed. Bow Island Lions Club, 1971. (61)

Snake Valley: A History of Lake McGregor and Area. Milo and District Historical Society, 1973. (110)

Spirit and Trails of Lac St. Anne. V. Davison, ed. The Alberta Beach Pioneers-Archives Society, 1982. (75)

Spurs and Shovels Along the Royal Line. M.I.P. History Book Society, 1979. (61)

The Sunny Side of the Neutrals. Bessie Smith, ed. The Association of Consort and District Seniors, 1983. (87)

Ten Dollars and a Dream. Mary Klein, ed. L.I.F.E. History Committee, 1977. (137)

Times to Remember. Joyce Burke and Janet Peers, eds. Acadia Valley Community Club, 1981. (75, 129)

Trails to the Bow: Carseland and Cheadle Chronicles. Carseland and Cheadle Historical Book Committee, 1971. (97)

Trails, Trials and Triumphs of Edberg and Community. Edberg Historical Society Book Club, 1981. (52, 71)

Under the Chinook Arch. Cayley Women's Institute, 1967. (11-12)

Vegreville in Review. Vegreville and District Historical Society, 1980. (74)

Vermilion Memories. The Vermilion Old Timers, 1967. (37, 65)

Wagon Trails Grown Over: Sexsmith to the Smoky. Sexsmith to the Smoky Historical Society, 1980. (4, 26)

Wheat Country: A History of Vulcan and District. Vulcan and District Historical Society, 1973. (73-74)

Wheatfields and Wildflowers: A History of Rycroft and Surrounding School Districts. Jean (Fraser) Rycroft, ed. Rycroft History Book Committee, 1984. (26)

Wheat Heart of the West. Irma Smith, Marshall Grant, and Hattie Chester, eds. Barons History Committee, 1972. ((41-43)

Where Friends and Rivers Meet: Flatbush and Surrounding Districts. B. Munteanu, ed. Flatbush Silver Threads Fifty Plus Club, 1986. (57)

Where the Prairie Meets the Hills: Veteran, Loyalist and Hemaruka Districts. Veteran Regional History, 1977. (26)

Winds of Change. Edgerton and District Historical Society, 1975. (71)

Yesterday and Years Ago: A History of Forestburg and District. Forestburg and District Historical Book Committee, 1983. (125)

Index

This index is not meant to be complete, but it should guide readers to various specific aspects of music in Alberta during the province's first century. I do regret that I have not been able to cite all individuals named in the text. Most citations refer to text, but occasionally the content indexed will be found in a photograph on the page given.